MIRRORED REFLECTION

Beyond the Surface: An Emotional Experience to Unleash Pain, Hope and Determination

DEBORAH L. JONES-ALLEN, PH.D., MBA

MIRRORED REFLECTION
Beyond the Surface: An Emotional Experience to Unleash Pain,
Hope and Determination
DEBORAH L. JONES-ALLEN, PH.D., MBA

Published by Pecan Tree Publishing, October 2011
Hollywood, Fl
www.pecantreepress.com

Library of Congress Control Number: 2010943299
ISBN: 978-0-9832078-1-8

PECAN TREE PUBLISHING

Hollywood, Fl.

www.pecantreepress.com

New Voices | New Styles | New Vision

Endorsements

This book is a must read for one who has found his or herself in the intensive care room of childhood hurt, low self-esteem and pain. I highly recommend this book because it gives the reader a touch of reality that many still encounter in this present age. Dr. Allen, I must say, - well done!

RANZER A. THOMAS, SR. PASTOR,
New Generation Baptist Church

Dr. Deborah Allen brings to the surface what was hidden and rooted deeply in her heart through the pages of this great literary work. She truly understands the revelation of God's word - that there is no condemnation to those who are in Christ Jesus. She is clearly transparent with the truth about her struggles, with acceptance and how she slowly triumphed over her fears. Her love for the Savior and those who may have been suffering from silent frustration and fear is evident; because she allows the reader to see her naked truth. I believe she talked with her Savior first and then this documented script is a result of her dialogue with Him. Her truth within the pages of Mirrored Reflection is a must read, and a transforming force in mirroring change if you would just look beyond the surface.

REVEREND YVONNE STRACHAN
Ministry in Motion Inc.
Miami Fl

Not many authors can express so candidly and yet intuitively their own personal struggles, and lift someone else out of a state of depression and despair. However, Dr. Allen has in her own transparent way done just that, in Mirrored Reflection. To my dear friend - well done.

DR. DEE GREATHOUSE, PRES/CEO
What About Me Ministries, International Inc.
Dr. Dee Greathouse Ministries, International Inc.

Table of Contents

Dedications

This book is dedicated to God's abiding love, mercy and divine grace. None of this would be possible without the healing power of a loving Savior; we must keep the focus on the Redeemer and His cross where all our debts were paid and sins were forgiven.

To my beloved husband Ronald—in all our years together, you have never ceased to amaze me. I call you beloved because of your wisdom, longsuffering, and gentleness. Your strength is the pillar of your character, you have allowed me to dream, throw tantrums, yet you calmly remain secure in our marital relationship. Your love towards our family has united us as one. I am blessed to share my life with you and submit to your loving hands. You have taught me how to love and be loved. For you are my priest, my friend, and my greatest inspiration!

This book honors my mother—Lillian Pecke who sacrificed love, so that her children would have a brick home. I also honor Adrian C. Jones, my grandson, who has witnessed so much at a young age; and who has allowed me to see my reflection and struggles through his life of emotional pain. It was through his experiences that my life began to unfold and the healing journey began for my entire family.

…. *"A CHILD SHALL LEAD THEM."* Jesus Christ challenged us when he said, "unless we become as a little child we would not see nor enter the kingdom of God."

I Feel You –

A Note from the Author

The apostle Luke, who was an outsider, identified with the least, the lost and the outcast. As a physician he and Jesus had much in common. They responded with compassion in time of need regardless of what others may have thought; or how they felt in the midst of a group, or heard silent whispers of disapproval. I am a part of that outsider group – much like you. There have been so many times in my life that I have felt excluded—as a child and as an adult. In both arenas, there have been many groups that shunned me and prevented my being a part of them. At times I found myself fighting just to survive the ridicule of the elite. The elite could be in family, or business and religious cultures. As my story unfolds, in the midst of rough terrains and dark valleys, you will find hope as the doors are opened and you are welcomed by God—through Jesus—to find mercy and grace behind pain and despair, rejection, feeling unwanted and unwelcomed. Today is the day that you will experience an unleashing and determination to pull up out of your situation and embrace a new hope as you go beyond the surface of a Mirrored Reflection. With God all things, including your healing and deliverance, are possible.

Preface

*"Sometimes it takes a painful experience to
make us change our ways."*

Proverbs 20:30 GNT

The thought that so many people shared similar, if not exactly the same experiences as I, had never occurred to me. It was very difficult for me to express in words, (especially in writing) my shame, guilt and fears; all firmly gripped and hidden within the secret places of my heart. There was a constant battle raging between my spirit and my mind. Worshipping Sunday after Sunday, year after year, as the accuser reminded me of my broken past. My life was out of order, as I failed to trust a loving Savior. I went to church seeking monetary gain, when I should have sought the Living Christ. The Word was on the surface yet my pain was deep down in my heart.

The thought never occurred to me that God would be able to rescue me from my emotional ills here on earth. In fact, I believed that one had to wait until they arrived in heaven before peace would claim their mortal body. This book is intended to speak softly to hearts and shout to the minds. As I share these deep intimate moments, personal struggles, and spiritual experiences that hindered me from accepting God as a Father, His Son's unconditional love and forgiveness in the raging storms and quiet moments of my life.

I hope this book will help not only you, but also your children's children overcome many of the emotional challenges they silently face on a daily basis as they seek refuge in the sanctuary of God. It took many years for me to understand that childhood hurts are just that -childhood hurts. When left untreated or unaddressed, they have the potential of developing into an array of unwelcomed personality disorders, emotional problems, and physical illnesses that interfere with your education, relationships, finances, and spirituality. Many childhood hurts, if not all of them, will pursue you well into your adult life.

The safest way to avoid the negative consequences of childhood hurts is to discover truth, seek help, and then make decisions to find peace with God, self, and with others. Failing to do so has the potential to create a cycle of destructive relationships, domestic violence, sexual/verbal and emotional abuse. The failure to deal with the negative can also create masking behind material possessions to relieve inward pains and sufferings. In this case, only the *Lord Himself will bring to light the hidden things of darkness, and will make manifest the counsels of the hearts.* (1 Corinthians 4:5)

I am sharing my personal determination to love and to be loved, as the healing leaves of scriptures (Revelation 22:2), authored texts, and personal affirmations guide you through your own journey of healing and hope. One person can alter their destiny by changing their present, and putting the past behind them. One person can heal by exposing the dark secrets of the past that have installed themselves as barricades and falsehoods in your mind and heart.

This book will not challenge the intellectual, in fact, it was written in a simple manner to challenge hearts and minds to find peace with God. My journey took me over rough terrains, through deep valleys of despair, fierce storms of depression, pitfalls of discouragement and over mountains of bitterness. My streaming tears as I wrote these words overshadowed the pain that was wedged deep within my heart. Nevertheless, it was in this writing that I decided to Let Go!

The major goal of this book is to bring an end to emotional suffering, particularly the tormenting pain that nibbles at our soul. This book also helps one to eliminate negative patterns, generational systems, and toxins that seek to pollute one's life; however, this will not be an easy task!

As an adult, it's not an easy assignment to confront a dark past in hopes of eliminating negative patterns and generational systems that seek to consume you with toxins that keep you in a barren place. This is a mere existence that's filled with unresolved hurts and fears that silently travel into your marriage, family, career and spiritual relationship. I hope to address these secret struggles and myriad emotions that are nestled within our human existence.

God's love is amazingly demonstrated as you release your issues in His hands. His peace is only a prayer away. In the midst of pain, there is hope and despite life adversities, you can live a victorious life. This is a spiritual principle and milestone that will release the determination to fulfill your purpose in life. Therefore, regardless if you see healing physically, feel it emotionally, or understand God's plans and purpose for your life spiritually, you must believe that He is in control of your future.

Life is filled with struggles, stressors, and fears and if not managed properly, issues of this life will transcend to our children's children. In addition, emotional hurts, unmet needs, and unresolved pains are all considered a roadblock that hinders us from loving others unconditionally, as we seek out unhealthy attachments. There is an opposite to life's adversities and that is when you know that there is an unlimited power source that accompanies hardships, tests and trials of life as an heir to the Father's kingdom. Something wonderful happens when you know this Truth. It's simple and so straightforward that it is difficult to understand- there is good in you! When a person recognizes that good is within them, it is then they are able to see themselves differently.

In order for many of us to move forward, we will have to journey back beyond immediate circumstances and painful memories. As recorded in the book of Genesis 3:12-13. This journey oftentimes must go back to the fall of the first family footstep. A place of blame, guilt and shame in the midst of paradise and peace, a place where we can accept and understand our true self of being created in God's image. This is the mirrored reflection that we all should seek to achieve.

Consider the making of a diamond. Many are sought after in distance lands and the majority are hidden within a dark outer core. At first glimpse, they rarely appear as a precious jewel to the one who discovers it, but deep within the dark casing, there is a hard clear valuable crystal. At first glance, it is impossible to detect its worth, but with a critical eye, one can see that the worth is nestled within the inner most part of the dark core. The point is, under all our brokenness and pain, there is a precious jewel that is priceless in our Father's eyesight.

As we allow the refiner's fire to burn off all our hurts and pains, this will allow us to move through the transformation process to become transparent in order to help someone else discover their purpose in God.

Allow the final process of change to occur by acknowledging the traumas of life; face the pain with someone you can trust, and depend on a greater power source to encase you with His unconditional love. You see you can't erase memories, the mind holds too many of them from your birth. What we can do is have enough of the Father's love to blanket us with a peace of mind in the midst of becoming who we were created to be; fearfully and wonderfully made before entering this toxic world of pain and suffering.

So let's journey together, as you begin your re-creation process. The fire must be turned up. The Master's private gem checks will inspect for leakage from Satan the accuser, who will attempt to tell you that your sins are many and God will not forgive you. Be aware of this during the transforming stage. Remember your debts were paid on the cross. When this happens, and it will, know that you are an overcomer by your testimony and the blood of the lamb. It is through your trails and tests that have allowed you to get this far by grace. Grace is a gift. Moreover, grace is what this generation needs in order to be set free from pain, debt, distress and the disconnect within. You must endure the final stages of your inspection before you are granted access to His kingdom. A loving Savior will escort you in the phase of refinement. Then you must be developed, polished and cut in order to humble you, as you lay before the King and all His glory. You and I are His lost treasures and without brokenness, it would be almost impossible to get a glimpse of what's in store for each of us in His pavilion of love, grace, and mercy. Beyond each break is a treasure ready to unleash great purpose in the Kingdom of God.

Now more than ever 'you' will need spiritual vision and divine revelation to recognize and understand these spiritual truths. As you sojourn with me, learn how to reposition your mind, will and emotions in God, through His son, Jesus. Everything was done at the cross and there is no one that the cross cannot reach. *"Therefore judge nothing before the time, until the Lord comes; and then shall every man have praise of God."* (1 Corinthians 4:5.KJV)

God has a higher purpose for our lives.

Blessings

Introduction

"Environment is but His looking-glass."

- James Allen, Author

It has been a long journey accepting that someone you love and trust can play a major role in your pains and fears. I saw secret fears open up as if it was my own reflection in the mirror, except it was an extension of my bloodline. That is when I had to move forward and take a proactive approach to face a possible dark past of shame and guilt. I need to make it very clear, looking back in no way means turning back. It is a method to discover and to seek answers to stop the cycle of madness in your life and take responsibility to seek out the help required to change generational patterns and false beliefs that prevent you from moving forward and living in peace in spite of the things that happen to you on the travels of life.

Regardless if your pain is emotional, physical, or verbal abuse, failure to seek help and take control of internal conflicts will only result in greater emotional pain that only passes onto the next generation. We are watching as generational gaps widen more so than ever. Society, the church and families are faced with generations living without boundaries, without moral conscience, and steeped in unhealthy and addictive behaviors. These behaviors escort irresponsibility, unhealthy family systems and further abuse that visits homes of three to four generations. The spiritual, physical and emotional cries that ring out from the land is alarming, almost an epidemic. Many (including this writer) are suffering from the evils of violence, anger, power and control, and emotional cracks that hinder their relationship with others, themselves and most of all—God. This is my way of sharing my story and how I was a recipient of God's unconditional love and forgiveness, redemption, and a true religious experience, shared with people from different walks of life.

I was able to find comfort and therapeutic benefits of healing for my soul. It took a minute before I realized I was not alone. There were others suffering as I was— in silence, as they cared for children who were filled with anger and rage because of a life of uncertainty. Many were struggling to remain in control of their homes, families, and personal lives. I was in disbelief of other's unwillingness to get professional or spiritual help to bring relief to their families and private lives. The warfare of screaming, shouting, and speaking in tongues could not control this sort of rage. In fact, it made things worse. Was love enough?

I pray that this writing engages you to seek out the truth behind the ills of family issues. It's time to heal past hurts in order to gain control over its pain. In doing so, you will embrace a magnificent future. A future filled with love, kindness, joy, peace, and longsuffering to care for the least and left out. *"There is no fear in love: true love has no room for fear, because where fear is, there is pain; and he who is not free from fear is not complete in love. (1 John 4:18 BEE)*

Loving God and His Son will require you to love Him in honesty to allow Him to love you back with such tenderness and care as you learn to cast all your cares upon Him. Not with a selfish love; one that hinders on material possession, aggression, fear, and control. I had to learn how to allow God to heal my wounds in order to receive freedom from all my years of life's hurts and painful experiences. A life rooted in destructive generational patterns through mirrored reflections of an emotionally battered child, which lead me to seek answers to my troubled past, broken trust, and issues which lead to revolving relationships.

Although my journey started years before I entered the school of psychology, I was desperate in my search for answers. I knew deep within, there was an emotional void in my life and unanswered questions to a dark and frightful past. My emotions were like a crystal glass, if you looked at me long enough, you could see my tears of pain and emotional hurts to the point of breaking. I was so fragile. The walls within my heart grew taller, as I grew angrier and more controlling of others' behaviors, and my life begin to spiral out of control.

In efforts to find peace and "truth", discoveries were made regarding life, relationships with people, and intimacy with God. It was in these discoveries that I realized there were many holes in my heart and only the Love of Jesus could heal the brokenness deep within me. His love is full of pity and grace. He is slow to anger, and great in mercy. Many times, He overlooks our evil, wrongdoings and sins because of ignorance. I believed for many years that God only kept a count of the wrong doings of my life, until I repented and changed my ways. It was then He remembered them no more. He gave me a new mind and heart. I even found favor in the Lord's sight. Healing is a process. Healing requires time and time is different for each individual. Today, I am healed by the precious blood and mercies of a loving Savior!

Healing requires you to learn to keep the focus off of others and keep your eyes on the Cross. The Cross is a place of perfect peace. When I learned about the true experience of the Cross, that's when my callous heart received relief from years of pain and hurt. I have to admit to you that this life is not pain free; you will have suffering and pain, but the suffering feels more like the thorn on a rose bush. The rose's beauty is far more precious

xx   Mirrored Reflection

than the pinch from the thorn. You become more aware that in the face of beauty are thorns, which come to remind us to handle them with care—such is Life. The world we live in has many struggles, trials, and decisions that will not always turn out to be filled with prosperity and blessings. Through it all, you can learn to control [or better handle] your emotional pain and avoid reacting to the circumstances in your life.

My home was surrounded with mirrors, but the image I saw was distorted because of the bumps and bruises from the troubles of this world. When I learned the truth of God's unconditional love and the truth about being created in His image, I desired a true relationship with His Son. This time I was willing to give Him my whole heart without any fears of it ever being broken or rejected again and that is when the light of His love shined in my soul bringing with it hope, promise, forgiveness, and peace to love again.

It is so important not to pass judgment on others. It is the Lord who will make clear the secret things of the dark. It is He that understands the intent of our thoughts and motives of the heart. Once the revelation of being created in the image of God was opened up to me, it was easier to understand being created in His image—I was fearfully and wonderfully made. God had great joy when He created us. This revealing truth, freed me from the things that dominated my thinking, emotions, and behaviors. Jesus can set people free from lifelong fears, shame, false guilt, anxiety, and lift the dark clouds of all emotional pain in a divinely directed moment.

Eager to learn the truth and know how to live in freedom, according to God's purpose and plans, gave me a new consciousness in understanding the inner workings of man and his suffering. Realizing the major ingredients in negative behaviors is a direct result of unresolved emotional pain, rejection, and unmet needs. It took courage to admit I could no longer do it with my own strength and in order to remain free and help my family, I would need the help of others, particularly, the help of the Holy Spirit and the people He placed in my life for such a time as this. I was able to get emotional release and peace, as I learned how to love my family and others unconditionally. Using biblical truths, wise counsel, and a change in my thinking gave me a newfound strength to endure many more hard places to come with confidence that the Lord was with me.

Everyday isn't peaches and cream, nor does the sun set on a fairy tale ending for my family. However, there is one thing for sure, my emotions are stable and the emotions of the children of my offspring are stabilizing as well. Negative circumstances are no longer in control of our destiny. We are able to self-regulate and better control our lives from emotional reactions. Together we are standing in battle with greater understanding, knowledge, and wisdom. The conquering King is fighting our emotional battles and in the end He wins!

Journey with me and learn how to seek out and ask for help. Discover your strengths, and identify your weaknesses by learning to admit and conquer conflicts within your body, mind, and soul. Learn how to identify, disarm, disable, and conquer self-defeating attitudes and mindsets that keep you dwelling in the wilderness land of "ifs" in your life; a spiritual deception and fatal flaw of fear and shame, designed to keep you locked and trapped behind a dark cell of pain.

Keys to the kingdom are waiting for you to unlock your destiny as you take greater steps towards a deeper walk spiritually and emotionally. Allow His Spirit to guide you to a balanced, satisfying and victorious life. My prayer is that you find your place in the city of God. It was not until I entered His city that I saw the whole picture of God's design for my life.

Understanding my temperament positioned me to understand my family and find balance as I humbly accepted my assignment in the Kingdom of God.

Jesus Christ has all the power and He alone can render the enemy powerless. He will restore your power and your sense of judgment. Truly, the mind of Christ will transform your life and open up options to a whole new world of love, trust and faith. The challenges of this world are not an easy thing to overcome, yet God's grace and mercy will keep you in times of adversity. My prayer is that everyone who reads this book finds healing for their own life as they find the courage to love unconditionally.

"Success is not measured by what you accomplish but by the opposition you have encountered and the courage with which you have maintained the struggle against overwhelming odds."

Orison Sweet Marden, Author

MIRRORED
REFLECTION

*Beyond the Surface: An Emotional Experience
to Unleash Pain, Hope and Determination*

Chapter 1

Dreams on Delay

"Hope deferred maketh the heart sick:
but when the desire cometh, it is a tree of life."

Proverbs 13:12 KJV

DREAMS ON DELAY

As I look back over my life, guilt and shame dominated and in fact were my best friends for such a long time. I was always struggling to gain the approval of others and to feel like I was somebody. Clearly, I believed that feeling would come through the acknowledgement and approval of others. Where did all of this originate?

As a child I could remember wanting the love of my mother and father. Yet, they could not be together for he was married to another woman. I knew something was wrong, because we only visited him at his barber shop and this went on for years. In the midst of this emotional ride, I was dealing with the secrets of being told not to let others know how a particular male close to our family loved me. Even now, I hold his identity in secret, because revealing it would hurt so many and possibly destroy my relationship with some. As a young girl I was molested by this person. The touch, in of itself, seemed to be okay. After all, he said he loved me – so I assumed it was okay. I can't tell you at what age I was penetrated, but what I do know is that the touch that eventually led to intercourse became a part of my secret world and just like an addict, sex was introduced to me as an escape mechanism and sex became my comfort.

Three baby daddies and years later, I thought all of those painful thoughts were erased from my memory, until my grandson entered my life. Not even my husband, Ronald was aware of my past. I often spoke to him in fragments – hiding even from the one with whom I shared the most sacred of vows. My relationship with Ronald was fun and fast. I had known him for years and he was my in between love most of my life. In other words, when one relationship ended for me or he had a desire to move outside of marriage, we would find each other. Until one day, I decided things needed to change, and so I put a demand on the table. He had to choose between his wife and me. That was the day that I lost my love. He chose to stay and raise his children over being in love with me. I respected him because I knew my mother had done the same thing.

Years later, when he and I finally got married, I did everything I could think of to make him pay for leaving me alone. This spiteful retribution lasted for about three years. According to him, living with me during that time, was a tormenting hell. I forced him to constantly prove his love, which included spending amazing amounts of money. I was making him pay to cover my inward pain – a pain that did not begin with him and could not be ended through him. I had to look good, because I never knew when I would run into his family and friends. I had to have the cars and the diamonds to prove that he was paying for his debt of betrayal. However, it came with a price on my part as well. I was drinking heavily and I was filled with an unforgiving soul. This interfered with our relationship.

My father used to say that it was better to have a drink than to do drugs, because one would last a little longer. When you wake up you will still have a drink. He would say. "Drugs cost more in the long run." What kind of advises was this? However, I trusted his words. You see, he loved me.

Many people have pain that they don't want you to know about, so they fake it from the outside and cover it up; this is what I was doing—covering up my pain. My world was framed by damaged emotions and what I observed from those near to me. I can remember going to church on Sundays after hearing my mom and stepfather yelling and screaming at each other. The arguments would be intense and threatening; but when we entered the sanctuary, as a picture-perfect family, the bickering would seem but a figment of my imagination. After an engaging worship service, the war zone would resume. A pressing on my heart suggested that what was being created in my marriage mirrored what I grew up with in my childhood. My mother resigned to provide a home for her children, rather than have the man she loved. My parents made it a Sabbath practice to fight on Sundays. Can you imagine that on the Lord's Day designed for rest; our home was painted in torment?

A few short years into our marriage, peace was becoming a fleeting thing as well. I was ready to run away from all of the demands that seemed important to me, the conflicts over the unrealistic demands, the counterfeit people who kept telling me it's my time to get what was mine and what I deserved. I was at the point of no return; my options were: move out or move away before people discovered the truth about my personal struggles. The mirror was showing a hard reflection yet again as a young woman I was ready to do the same thing that my mother had done. She moved to the more rural areas of Florida leaving her husband in Miami. I was about to repeat the cycle. Although, my desire was to have a husband at my side, my reality was that I was pushing my very independent personality into a marriage. It was a battle fought with determination and lots of prayer to save my marriage and put a detour in a cycle that promoted loneliness, despair, and sacrifices at the risk of emotional and mental health. The prayer had finally opened the door to a new season of possibilities and I was looking forward to finally escaping with my husband.

* * *

My youngest daughter was in her senior year of high school and had successfully passed the Florida Comprehensive Assessment Test® (FCAT) which is part of Florida's overall plan to increase student achievement by implementing higher standards[1]. There was so much fear attached to it that I called it Fear cat. I was so excited about her bright future. I knew how much of a struggle it was for her. She is smart, but she has her own way of doing things and that sometimes makes things challenging in the least. For her, passing this test was a great accomplishment and I was proud of her. Now all of my children had met my expectations of completing high school. (I had no doubt. I just worried.) With her graduation at hand that meant in two more years it would be off to the countryside with my husband.

I was ready to embrace the fresh crisp winter mornings, steaming hot summers and long walks in the autumn leaves! Everyone knew of our plans to retreat to the country, since it was all we talked about. Deep in our hearts, we knew none of the children would want to follow us to such a boring place and that was great. My husband was preparing for retirement and I had envisioned working for the school board in the town to which we were moving. I envisioned long winter breaks, spring breaks, lavish summer picnics, and traveling around the world. What an ideal place to spend our time, in the country, a home away from home, far and removed from the fast pace and stress of a growing and forever changing cultural landscape like South Florida. Don't get me wrong we love South Florida, we just needed a change of pace and I wanted to be alone with my husband.

One morning, while getting ready for Sunday worship service, I realized that there was something particularly different about this Sunday. I longed for my heart's desire to be fulfilled. A dream that I treasured within my inner soul and I felt it was time for my dreams to manifest. Along with my husband, the man of my dreams, he would carry me away from the cares of this world. I could envision him carrying me in his arms across the threshold of our new country home. The double doors would open to a flowing entrance, with palm trees standing tall, ready to welcome us.

My heart was racing as my thoughts were embracing quiet yet resounding whispers from God saying, "It's not time yet." I turned a deaf ear to the voice of God. I only wanted to hear the loud sounds in my ears from a worship song that goes something like, "the best is yet to come, and the latter will be greater." Then, my eyes slowly moved upward to a note that I had placed on my mirror to remind me of God's timing.

"And let us not be weary in well doing: for in due season we shall reap, if we faint not."

Galatians 6:9KJV

Several months later, a cry for help changed my life forever. I was about to be forced to ask myself if I was willing to delay a peaceful life in the country to take an active role in a life that was ripe with nightmares, pain and suffering. Why would the gift giver take His gift and a beautiful dream from me? A dream I had envisioned for years.

One letter shattered every plan and thrust us into unfamiliar and questionable territory. My grandson Adrian was in trouble. He had been taken out of his mother's home and placed in foster care. It was a traumatic experience for him; one that only escalated from what we would later find out had been many traumatic experiences. Parents that were constantly fighting, feeling threatened, feeling afraid and rejected. He failed to adjust in foster care and without his prescribed medication his negative behaviors escalated and my young grandson, still years away from being a teenager was poured into the state juvenile justice system.

This was not in my dreams and I wanted the original dream back—now! I cried and prayed and cried and prayed. While some may feel I was being selfish, the truth of the matter is, I did not want to change my plans to care for a troubled child. My days of parenting were over. Or so I thought. Still I had to endure like a good soldier who had enlisted in battle for the Lord in order to help my grandchild. I knew Satan was up to something and he was coming to steal, kill, and destroy my plans and yet another generation in my family. For months, we made multiple trips to Jacksonville, Florida from South Florida, attending one court hearing after another. The department that regulates foster care in the state, had no record of Adrian (my grandson) having family outside of his parents. His mother for many reasons did not disclose the information; and though Adrian voiced it, his voice went unheard. The state questioned our filings to gain temporary custody of a child that no one else wanted. Part of me honestly was okay with that, after all, he was interfering with my plans.

I was experiencing severe emotional discomforts at the time and I did not like any of the feelings going through me. I questioned God about my future in moments of discomfort, yes, I questioned God. I asked Him, why was he allowing this to happen to me? What happened to the dream- life promised to me? Was it my fault this happened? Was I being selfish? What did I do to deserve this lot in life? In the midst of God's promises—anger, bitterness and resentment were keeping me from having peace with God. My worst fears were keeping me in bondage and constrained my ability to display unconditional love without realizing this child was as fearful as I was.

What I thought was going to be a month or so, felt more like chasing the wind in my hand. After paying lawyers to help sift through his early years and much paper work and psychological tests; we discovered that Adrian was dealing with more than we were willing to acknowledge. None of us knew how the story would end and it was time to face the truth and commit to caring for a child whose world was filled with trauma and emotional pain from young parents who failed to seek the support of their family. His life was filled with emotional garbage and leftovers from a broken mother and father. A child who had suffered through domestic violence, post traumatic stress disorder and was living well below his expected educational, social, and psychological levels. I would look at all of the records, the details of various occurrences and feel conflicted. He was a part of me. Could I have helped him sooner? Could it be that he would live all of his life based on the labels of man? Was it his fault? Then the Lord responded in a question ever so softly, "What was family for, if not to help each other when they are in trouble, especially in difficult times?"

Adversity was about to become a part of my daily life. Guilt and shame became my friends again, taunting me because I had potentially not done my part as a grandmother. You see before all of this came to pass, I made a promise to Adrian that I would check on him every Sunday at 4: 00 pm. It was a promise I failed to keep because I had my own stuff going on. When life has you jammed in, it is difficult to breathe and remember a sense of duty – even to a child who needed to be checked on at times. I was being reminded that this was in part my fault. If I had fulfilled one promise, could I have helped keep this emotionally challenged child from derailing?

The back and forth trips, battles in court and financial issues were just the beginning of what quickly became the wildest rollercoaster ride of our lives. Months past and I was at my wits end. I felt like I was not getting any real relief for my grandson from traditional counseling. Nothing was working with him. Nothing seemed to help the outbursts of every conceivable kind. The entire family was now sharing in the life of a child's suffering. Trust was a major concern for him. It was time to face the truth. I had to learn to live with a challenged and hurting child, who learned at such a young age to guard his heart and refused to trust even those closest to him, his family.

Late one night while sitting at the dining room table, reading and praying for answers, the Holy Spirit whispered gently, "You have been through this before –remember." Then my daughter flashed across my mind; and I recalled how difficult the emotional connection was in our relationship, and this was my last attempt to change our unnatural affection. Determined to prevent a repeat in history, the Spirit provoked me to the computer. I searched and explored until two in the morning, feeling almost defeated, when suddenly my eyes fixed on Reactive Attachment Disorder (RAD).

Reactive Attachment Disorder (RAD) is a mental health disorder in which a child is unable to form healthy social relationships, particularly with a primary caregiver. Often children with RAD will seem charming and helpless to outsiders, while waging a campaign of terror within the family. RAD is frequently seen in children who have had inconsistent or abusive care in early childhood, including children adopted from orphanages or foster care. Physical, emotional, social, mental, and spiritual health are all affected by RAD. These children learn that the world is an unsafe place and find it difficult to trust that others can take care of their needs and believe they must take care of themselves. Because they could not rely on parents to keep them safe during those first months or years, they have learned that adults are uncaring, rejecting, unreliable, and violent or absent. These children believe they can stay safe by pushing adults away, making them angry, manipulating them—anything to distance themselves from adults physically and emotionally. Their defiant behaviors, bad tempers, and poor peer relationships also characterize them. Behaviors can also escalate to stealing, lying, destruction of property, and a lack of conscience. In many cases, these children have behavioral and learning problems in school. To expect the child to function as a typical child when his normal development was completely stunted back in infant -toddlerhood is not rational. In fact, it becomes a developmental impossibility-plaguing therapist and parents who try with a lifetime of uncertainty and emotional distancing. We must view such children in a manner that is not common and provide them with an environment conducive to a corrective regulatory experience (Post 2001)[2].

I was tired. Adrian was taking my life to a whole new level of patience, temperance and understanding. He lacked self control, was verbally abusive and physically destructive. Ronald found himself, not wanting to be home, which meant that I had to deal with him alone far too often. My husband was being called to the school almost daily because of Adrian's behavioral problems. And I was playing counselor constantly instead of being a loving and supportive grandparent. I could not be both. , What was I to do? He was destroying my home. And there were times I would say if he hit my mirrors, if he kicked those doors, if he slammed something into those walls one more time—I was going to have to make a choice -my home or this child. He was not safe and neither was I. So we were at an impasse.

Now I was not happy and my emotions were out of control. I was offended that he was not respecting me as a grandparent. I could feel myself growing bitter towards him. How could I not like or trust him? He was part of me. The words of his diagnosis could not be discarded; the effects of it were beginning to disturb my family more. Now I was fearful of my own safety. I begin to read the stories of families traumatized by children with RAD as I was making plans to defend those I loved just in case his lack of conscience got the best of him. I moved all the knives from his view to keep us safe, if only but in my mind.

* * *

As I traveled this lonely journey of faith, I experienced God purifying my sinful heart. A heart filled with unmet needs of fears, guilt, and shame. I felt my husband should be a part of my journey, He was here, but I wanted Ronald to rescue me by requesting that we send Adrian back, so we could move on with our lives. I was ready to return him to the system that I fought to get him out of, not knowing God's plan and what he was doing in my life. Many times I was angry that my husband would not or could not travel this road with me. I learned that it was all in my perception. I would be angry with my husband feeling like he was deserting me at night, leaving me with a child I feared would wake up and attack me. Yet, it was my fear creating a non-existent situation. Ronald was not deserting us, he was merely going to work as he always had and needed to do. I had to realize that I needed to combat the negative emotions that were driving this child and that were very definitively driving me and running the situation in my home.

In an interesting twist, one occurrence unleashed a different perspective on things. One evening as my grandson was taking a bath, the grandma in me thought to check in on him and assure he was washing all of his body parts, I opened the door abruptly and without knocking, startling him.

"Grandma! What you doing?!" he exclaimed.

After a complete check of his body, I began to close the door behind me, and I suddenly noticed these toy soldiers with guns strategically positioned around the bathroom. I asked what were they for and what did their positioning mean, He told me they were protecting him and preventing anyone from coming to see him without his clothes. I could not understand initially how toy soldiers could protect him. I hurried to my husband and told him what I had witnessed. I began to connect his need for protection, (no matter how far out the means seemed to me), with the possibilities of what could have happened to him. What did he experience that he was not sharing? I called in more counselors. I had to know. My husband just shook his head in disbelief of the possibility of child sexual abuse. We were both grateful and relieved to find out that our worse fears, were only those and – thank God – he had not been molested. However, he had witnessed something with his mother and that proved more traumatic for him. So while he understood having to be with his grandparents, he also felt out of control and out of place. He felt that because he was with us, his mother was in danger. You see he was, as he shared with me one night during dinner, not there to protect her and keep "it" from happening again. He was out of his protective position. He was out of his home. He was fighting everything and everybody because he was lost, hurt, confused, scared and yet he could not communicate any of that. When he did communicate, it was abusive and threatening.

With all of this now a part of my life and my energy, I had grown weary. I was tired of yelling. I was tired of reacting to his outbreaks. I was tired of explaining things. I was tired of trying to figure him out. I was tired of pretending that everything was okay or that I enjoyed caring for this child. I remember in the height of this life of turmoil 'what will he do today,' a new caseworker made a home visit. After the drill of giving his history again and asking myself again isn't reading the case files part of the job; I provided her with what I thought were sufficient reasons and details to get additional treatment for him and help for me. About 45 minutes into the interview, she advised me very calmly to do something that strangely angered me.

"Mrs. Allen, I know you want to help your grandchild, but trust me the best thing you could do for him is give him back. He is not ready to live with you or can he appreciate this nice home you have here. If he wants to destroy your things or you feel in danger, the next time just call the police and have him taken away. The worst thing that can happen is you will be embarrassed to have your neighbors see the police at your home."

I looked at her, smiled and said, "You may be right and I would be embarrassed, but this is my grandchild and I love him. I don't want him to live in a group home, that's the reason all this started. The system did not help to find us and his mother said we did not exist. Yes, I want help but not to have the child committed, taken to juvenile again or to another group home. I want a break; some help…"

He had his problems behaviorally and emotionally, but he was not psychotic. What was she thinking? I signed her home visit form and said have a nice day as I showed her to the front door. Now it was back to the drawing board. My search was on to find help and respite. I honestly believe if government care sponsored better or more respite for grandparents, more of us would consider keeping children who need special care and are high risk. If we are burnt out who will help us? We both were in need, he wanted his mother regardless of the pain, and I wanted my peace back.

Amazingly, in the thick of the adjustment, diagnosis, turmoil and more, God appointed two spiritual warriors to support me and become my new friends as they traveled with me until it was time for them to relinquish their positions as spiritual companions. Sorrow and longsuffering were their names. They were strong and full of Godly-wisdom. Sorrow and longsuffering gave me greater insight on how patience must be allowed to do her perfect work in each of us if we are to become mature and complete in wisdom and knowledge and lacking nothing. It is all about giving God glory from our trampled-on lives.

James Allen wrote in his book, *As a Man Thinketh*, "Suffering is always the effect of wrong thought in some direction. It is an indication that the individual is out of harmony with himself… the sole and supreme use of suffering is to purify, to burn out all that is useless and impure."[3] There were new lessons for me to learn, and the curriculum was designed by a loving God, for me, His child. I was the one who need a heart change. My family was looking to see what I would do next. What lesson was I to learn, that I keep failing the test. The diagnosis of RAD was ringing out in my mind so often, which it became a part of my thoughts.

My thinking was about to change on how my destiny was the divine will of God on earth. God was no longer the God of blessings and prosperity. He wanted the best for us from the day He created us in his image. *"I know what I'm doing. I have it all planned out—plans to take care of you, not abandon you, plans to give you the future you hope for"* (Jeremiah 29:11 Message). Sorrow and longsuffering was traveling with me to challenge my thinking about God's will and to learn the true meaning of His will for my life.

> *He does all according to the counsel of his will. We often do not know our own thoughts, nor know our own mind, but God is never at any uncertainty within himself. We are sometimes ready to fear that God's designs concerning us are all against us; but he knows the contrary concerning his own people, that they are thoughts of good and not of evil; even that which seems evil is designed for good. His thoughts are all working towards the expected end, which he will give in due time. Though it last long, it shall not last always.-. He will give them, not the expectations of their fears, nor the expectations of their fancies, but the expectations of their faith, the end which he has promised and which will turn for the best to them. This shall be in answer to their prayers and supplications to God (Matthew Henry)*

"You must be the change you want to see in the world"

Mahatma Gandhi

It was time to see through the eyes of a child, in order to understand God's truth regarding unconditional love, forgiveness, and giving without conditions. It was difficult for me to understand how sorrow could have a purpose in the plans of God for my life, but if nothing else; my family learned to draw closer to a loving and compassionate Savior. It was these moments of promptings from the Holy Spirit that I sought out divine knowledge and wisdom from the Scriptures. I allowed the Word of God in to help me discover true healing through unconditional love and forgiveness. A lesson that if not learned will repeat itself until I was ready to make the grade.

If healing was going to be a part of the process, it was now time to make a commitment to God and stand in the gap spiritually, physically, and emotionally. God has made us what we are, and through His Son, He has established us for a life of purpose. A life to help, guide and serve others. Moreover, at the same time he has prepared inner healing to the giver of life in the process of helping others. A life of service he has prepared for each of us to do. A life that brings healing to those around us, as we share in the healing process of God's magnificent plans, overflowing with hope, peace, longsuffering, and then the true blessings will come.

Although my relationship with my grandson is moving forward and our family is growing stronger in our faith, there are times that I have to keep reminding my husband and everyone involved in his life that lying about the obvious, learning lags and poor peer relationships seems to be an issue for him. In addition, this is only for a season, because I believe God's Word, that healing is for everyone because of the cross. The spirit declares that we are over comers, and something good is in all of us. As we pray for a spirit of endurance power to care for this generation and the Spirit of God to equip and place people in our lives who care about his total well-being,(physically, emotionally, educationally, socially and spiritually). God's love will continue to strengthen us with His divine grace. Our labor in love must be gentle toward all, as the Holy Spirit qualifies us daily to teach and instruct families in mildness. Hoping that they may come back to their proper senses and pull out from the snare of the devil, seeing that they have been caught off guard to do the evil one's will. But know this; adversity is not the enemy, we can have victory as quoted by Winston Churchill," I have nothing to offer but blood, toil, tears and sweat." In times of war, we must be prepared to preserve our posterity. For in the last days critical times will come, times so hard that many will give up and not want to deal with their own. It gives me comfort to know this battle is not mine, it's the Lord's. The good news gospel changes lives. This is his work and I believe God is in control. I have been given a test. I admit I don't have all the answers, but I will continue until I pass and proceed to the next level. Just like fishermen were turned to disciples and promoted through their sufferings and sorrow to apostles. So it is with us. We must not give up in doing what is good, for in due season, we shall reap if we do not tire out.

Chapter 2

My New Friends— Sorrow and Suffering

"We may make our plans, but God has the last word."

Proverbs 16:1 GNT

MY NEW FRIENDS -SORROW AND SUFFERING

On my way up to enjoying my life by attending social functions, joining professional groups, and traveling to places that are now placed on hold; I began to understand the words of Jeremiah 29:11, *"For I know the thoughts that I think toward you, saith Jehovah, thoughts of peace, and not of evil, to give you hope in your latter end" (ASV)*. I had twisted the Word of God to suit my own needs, which was, "eat, drink, and be merry for tomorrow you die." I was convinced that it was my time to shine. I did my volunteering projects, helped within my community, and gave financial gifts to the church. I just knew my responsibility of caring and raising children was over. I was a 21st century grandparent. I had already raised my children, completed my education, and was working on a new career. I was finished with that parenting phase of my life and it was time to *inherit* the things of God; according to my understanding.

Sailing in familiar waters, my focus was on me and in the middle of my journey, my ship decided to change its course. The view was unclear and my destination had not yet been given to me by God. I was confused about God's plans for my life. I was looking for a get-out-of-adversity pass from The Father. Instead, adversity was about to teach me an important lesson about life and build my character in the process. I have to admit to you, it was very difficult not knowing or understanding God's plan for my life, as I was no longer in control.

In order to understand the changes that were going on in my life, I had to embrace the scriptures, listen to the voice within my heart and follow His instructions. Sitting still in meditation, the Book of Proverbs answered the mysteries God had for my life. Three verses helped me to remain focused and gave me the strength to embrace my daily adversities.

You may think everything you do is right, but the Lord judges your motives.

Ask the Lord to bless your plans, and you will be successful in carrying them out.

You may make your plans, but God directs your actions.

Proverbs 16:2, 3, 9 GNT

So, where did I go wrong? Did I use a dream to escape a struggling marriage? Deep inside I was tired of being a parent. It was time for me to be free. I saw a generation of grandparents traveling and having fun and it was my time. Did I get the blessing of God to relocate or was I ready to throw in the towel of parenting? Feeling free of responsibility on the outside, and yes I was pretending, debts were flowing out of the ceiling. I had the fake it until you make it mindset, all the time I was longing and thirsting for love deep within my soul. Still, there was no one with which to share these struggles. Most people had sized me up and judged me according to what they observed from the outer man being projected. My emotional walls were high and still no one took the time to really ask me—*truly* how was I doing. Oh, yeah, people questioned me about my family. If everything was well, I smiled and held hands with my husband in public. So they saw a picture perfect couple whose lives were all but that. The stress was building from caring for my grandchild, as my husband was growing tired of being awaken during the day after working all night. I could not let the church people know that I was tired. I could hear my pastor, "keep up the good work- Adrian looks good" while in the midst my heart was aching.

I managed to remain polite and wear a holy smile, while my emotions were in conflict with my spirit man. I was angry and longing for a compassionate church member to help me cross the dark places of my life. There were many topics about me that I refused to talk about for fear of being rejected or criticized about my past. I understood testimony; however, my pain was just that—pain! My pain was covered with a band-aid that was about to fall off. My past was catching up with me, so much so that even during worship services, I felt like I was about to lose my mind.

One particular Sunday, my intimate worship was somewhat different. I felt as if was in the sanctuary all alone. My eyes were closed as a red heart with a black hole in the middle of it suddenly appeared. I thought it was strange, that the Spirit would show something like this to me. I loved the Lord and I was faithful in my worship to Him. I could feel the tears streaming down my face. His Spirit was ministering to me with a soft gentle voice. "I love you and there is more I have for you. Will you give me your whole heart?" I could not believe what was happening to me. Could He be telling me that my worship was not enough and that my expression of love for Him required more? Although this time my tears were refreshing, somehow my heart was telling me that I was about to have the Father remind me of His love and finish work at the cross.

Jesus himself, the Holy One of Israel had come to heal me with His love. I was excited about what was happening to me. He came to heal me. How could this be possible? I was strong! I was tough and I managed to keep my emotions in check when I was out in public. Still, Jesus knew the truth about me and the private conditions of my heart. I could not hide my pain and fears from him any longer, besides, He knew all about me. He knew that I failed to trust those who were around me. He knew my trust had been violated. He knew my life was void of trusting relationships. My secrets were the source of my emotional distress and discontentment. The Carpenter was removing the "condemnation" sign from my heart and it hurt to have this message remove. I was weakened by the thought of having my life open for all to see. What if my family found out about me? Would they love me still- unconditionally? Could it be possible that this was my heart? Somewhere deep within it was a black hole filled with unresolved pain and fear. A past that I thought was so distressful, that I had blocked it from others with a CONDEMNED sign posted, hiding the hole in the secret place of my heart. It was preventing me from having a trusting relationship with my heavenly Father, the giver of love. Now the time had come for the Lord to take away my fears and fill me with His love. He was preparing me for my final washing to take away the things that kept my mind enslaved.

The day wore on me. I felt refreshed, excited, and exhausted from this unusual worship experience and visitation from the Lord. Still I longed for His presence and to know precisely what I was clutching. What was keeping me tied to my past? I knew that if I searched the scriptures and questioned an elder, answers could be found, but instead of finding answers to my questions, I was given more words. Words like: "Trust in the Lord", "Wait on God," He's an on time God," and "Lean not to your own understanding." What was wrong with people? Was there not anyone that could interpret what the Lord was telling me? I wanted to know what the black hole meant for my life.

I must have dozed off, only to be awakened by a thunderous voice from an apparent dream. I sat on the bed in complete silence; shaken by the memories of climbing a ladder and falling. I was headed straight to the top of a long straight and narrow ladder. I was moving very quickly almost reaching the top, when suddenly my feet began to slip. My hands quickly fastened to both sides of the ladder, when I started to fall, taking the ladder down with me. Before I knew it, I was looking upward toward a hole in the ceiling and thinking what was wrong with me using this type of ladder. It had no support and I was too heavy for it. As I was lying on the ground, a voice yelled out from the background, "Next time use the stairs." As I turned and looked away, out of nowhere a winding staircase was on the other side of me with people standing waiting on me to come and join them.

It took some time for me to discern that the thunderous voice came from God and the people waiting for me was my family; a family God had entrusted to my care. A ladder taking me straight to the top but I had to be ready to take the fall and face the fact that I was willing to trade my family for selfish reasons, instead of facing my hardships and failures that were so eager to travel with me. Did something go wrong or did I forget to ask God to bless my plans? Traveling was something I always wanted to do; it had become my heart's desire. If I stopped and attended to my family needs they would interfered with me achieving my aspirations, which were already set into motion. I didn't need any approval from others for this. Besides, they never told me the truth anyway, particularly those who said they loved me.

PURE MOTIVES

Was I seeking attention by excelling in my education? Could it be that I was searching for the three A's in my life, *approval- acknowledgement- accomplishment, and* in my search was I hoping that these things would come from those I love, my family? Maybe it was time for God to search me and unravel many unanswered questions that pursued me over the years. The truth is that I was moving so fast, I hadn't had time to deal with my past. It was time for me to go under God's microscope. He was about to test my motives, altering my plans, and accurately assess me for a future filled with hope and expectancy according to His will, plans and purpose.

Unknowingly, I had allowed fear, insecurity, and a painful past to force themselves on me. In return, they drove me to attain selfish goals at the cost of almost losing my entire family. Neither vocational nor educational successes were worth me sacrificing my marital relationship and risking the loss of my children or grandchildren. It sprang from my need to search outside of God's love. Scripture teaches that man looks at the outward appearance, but God judges the intent of the man's heart.

How could God do this to me, He knew I loved Him and He was the only one on whom I could truly *depend.* In spite of all this, there remained a pain nestled deep within my heart. It felt as if someone was stealing His love from me. I couldn't stand the thought of being another wounded person in the family of God.

I had convinced myself that I was working for the Lord in the marketplace of healthcare. My mother did it and never was criticized, so why couldn't I do the same? I sincerely believe that what I was doing put me in right standing with God. I was in the vocation He had instructed me to enter. I was sharing my personal story with those whom He instructed me too. I was serving both the young and old. Some people, who crossed my path, simply needed a little emotional attention during moments of desperation and frustration. You know, like times when you just need someone to push you through a tight place in life? I shared with strangers that God loved them *as is,* but His love for them was too powerful to leave them in the same condition. His love is unconditional without accusing, judging or condemning anyone of their past mistakes, faults or failures.

As I reflect over my life, it was apparent that my time was used helping the least, lonely, and left out; those who others rejected and put on the short list within our gracious society. If anyone was doing his or her part, it was me, so what was the problem with me using the ladder? My life was busy enough and I was ready to try something new. As far as I was concerned, travel plans were the only thing on my mind. Abruptly, my life had an "all about me" tone. Then out of nowhere, a nudging pierced through my heart as a soft whisper echoed in my ears, "Get ready to receive your blessing!" These words were as clear, as the sun shining in mid July! These are the words I longed to hear from God. "Receive your *Blessing!*"

Little did I know that the gift to be received was the gift of "unconditional love" and the Gift Giver was going to be the One to give it. I had no idea that the best candidates to work in the Kingdom of God were the rejected, bruised, battered, and the one suffering within their private lives. We must be careful that our motives are right in the eyes of God. I lacked full respect for the Holy Spirit's power to teach me all things, according to His knowledge and righteousness, so I tampered with His power. One day in a zealous attempt to use the knowledge of the Holy Spirit, I sought after Him, unlearned and ignorant about the things of God. I asked the Holy Spirit to teach me about Jesus. Instantly, I felt a sharp pain in my side, a pain so sharp it radiated throughout my back. I fell to the floor yelling out for help. No one answered me. I was all alone. The pain was so great that Fancy (my Maltese) looked at me with amazement. Bent over and lying on the floor in pain and agony, the Holy Spirit spoke, "The pain! Know the pain! The pain at the Cross, the same pain that a loving Savior suffered, so that the world may have eternal rights to the blessings you are seeking."

How could He share this type of suffering with me? My relationship with Him was not like that—or so I thought. I did not feel worthy to share in His sufferings. Was it today, that the Gift Giver Himself was giving me a lesson in unconditional love? I felt His pain and that was a lesson I will never forget. My daughter always said, "One day someone is going to bring you down off that white horse you are riding."

I was clearly able to understand, that the intent of our hearts is what God deals with; therefore, I will boast in nothing but the Lord and I will do it with all humility. The death on the cross was for mankind to know how a loving Savior died because of His love toward them. I believe He wants our hardened hearts to change into compassionate people, loving even when we hurt. In that moment, it was no longer okay to have a "good idea with wrong motives." If I truly wanted God's blessings, then I had to be willing to give God glory and praise in all things.

Our motives must be pure in the eyesight of God.

Because of this, let us have a strong desire to come into that rest, and let no one go after the example of those who went against God's orders. For the word of God is living and full of power, and is sharper than any two-edged sword, cutting through and making a division even of the soul and the spirit, the bones and the muscles, and quick to see the thoughts and purposes of the heart. In addition, there is nothing made which is not completely clear to him; there is nothing covered, but all things are open to the eyes of him with whom we have to do. Having then a great high priest who has made his way through the heavens, even Jesus the Son of God; let us be strong in our faith. For we have not a high priest who is not able to be touched by the feelings of our feeble flesh; but we have one who has been tested in all points as we ourselves are tested, but without sin. Then let us come near to the seat of grace without fear, so that mercy may be given to us, and we may get grace for our help in time of need. (Hebrews 4: 11-16 BBE)

All of us desire the things of God, material things, health, peace, and joy. In order to receive the divine things of God, our motives must be sincere towards Him. He knows all things in heaven, on earth and in the deepest parts of the dark world. Because He knows all things, He wants to change our course in life from a destructive path of sin and remorse to His will and His original design for our lives. Now having matured in some things, I am able to understand more clearly God's purpose and plan for my life.

I am watching in awe as His transformational process and inner healing comes to my body, mind, and soul. I now know for sure, that without Him we can do nothing. God is radically changing my life, my family's lives, and others around me personally, professionally, within and out of the body of Christ. Every now and then, He has to cut back some of my ways that are not pleasing to Him. Especially, if my life takes on a direction that will prevent me from doing His will. I believe the fruit we are destined to bear, if we are Jesus' followers, must be shaped in His unconditional love. *"No greater love"* is so easy to recite, especially on Sundays. I don't know about you, but I find myself reciting it like my ABC's. Yet, when I ponder my heart and mind on Monday, will a man put his *own* life on hold for another to have life?

Suddenly, the meaning of my dream was clear. I was living in a fast-paced society, where the focus is turned on self, vanity, and money. Money was not wrong, because in this world you need money in order to survive; however, it became wrong when obtaining money became my ultimate focus and prevented me from having fun with my loved ones. While putting intimate relationships on hold, the meaning of family had become a vapor in the night's air. My children were no longer held close to my heart but instead had become a constant worry on my anxious mind. That's when I knew I was falling from the grace of God, failing as a wife, mother, and grandmother to those He had entrusted to me. My life was out of order.

I searched to see if families in my sphere of influence were still smiling, having fun, enjoying each other, spending time together, and experiencing the power of God's love. However, what I found was a sad commentary for such an advanced society; they were worse off than I was. Compliments became complaints and pleasantries about children or grandchildren had become *"Little Chucky"* horror stories. This was far and removed from how God had intended anyone to live his or her life. His intent was not a life filled with regret and worry, topped with a negative outlook regarding our posterity. Most people around me were blaming their children for not being responsible adults. Thus, they were leaving grandparents to care for grandchildren in their prime of life. All of us knew the scriptures particularly; the Kingdom of God is love, peace, joy and the power of the *Holy Ghost.* Yet, we were all struggling to attain unconditional love.

It was apparent that there was an urgent need to seek out creative and innovative approaches to motivate and educate those around us, but how could I focus on the people around me when, I had similar issues in my own family? Where did I begin to lose focus from my family? When did I start putting my life before others? Yes, my heart had a flaw deep within and it was time that I embraced the changing society and a generation that required unconditional love from those who lived in God's kingdom.

A generation that has the courage to challenge my beliefs and my ability to love them with the unconditional love of Christ, a changing and challenged generation that lives *"fast and furiously."* Moreover, a generation that questions my authority while challenging me to see that they are capable of loving, if given an opportunity. A generation that could sense emotional suffering from a mile away and it's this generation that fails to trust even those closest to them.

I realize that it is this generation that motivated me to search my heart, re-evaluate my spiritual life and learn the truth about a loving, forgiving and merciful Savior. It is through a loving Savior, that these deviant and powerful spirits of anger, control, and fear will be driven out from our family and society in which we live.

The more I learned of His unconditional love the more I accepted His Word as truth. It was not easy to go back and search out the fearful things that were keeping me from having a life of peace and joy. It took courage and His unconditional love to change the situation in my home and family. By accepting His love, I was ensured that the unwelcomed guests of anger, control, and fear were able to leave their home deep within the darkness of my heart. It is this love, which comes from our *heavenly Father* that will enable you to love yourself from the inside out, drive out hate, heal a broken heart and redeem a shattered past.

Chapter 3
Stability and Uncertainty

*"Darkness cannot drive out darkness; only light
can do that. Hate cannot drive out hate; only
love can do that."*

Dr. Martin Luther King, Jr.

STABILITY AND UNCERTAINTY

Sunday mornings around my house were amazing. I looked
forward to my mother softly knocking on doors singing her
love songs to God. "Rise-shine- give- God your glory –Oh- give
God your glory." "This little light of mines, I'm going to let it
shine-let it shine- let it ." Then she would thank God for her
family. If that was not enough to wake me from my night's
sleep, the smell of crisp bacon flowing through the air sure did.
I had to hurry and dress because her oatmeal and cheese toast
were waiting for her family on the table.

We had a family motto, "A family that prays together stays
together." Sitting around the table waiting until Deac finished
his long prayers; the food would often grow cold before he
finished his prayer sermon. The family would all sit together
before going to church. This was a family tradition. Sometimes
my mother would send us to church with Deac, especially if
she had to work, but most of the time the family went to

church together. Deac was my mother's husband and her third baby daddy as well. Does this all-sound familiar? In addition, in his home we were all considered his children. If we called him anything but daddy, he would bring out the belt and a speech to show us how much he was providing for Lillian's children.

Our home was beautiful, with plenty of room for other family members who chose to seek refuge during turbulent times in their lives or severe stormy weather. Helping others was a part of my mother's life and despite helping others have a safe place to live, her life was filled with sorrow and pain. Sunday mornings were filled with the love of Jesus and Sunday nights were engulfed with fussing and fighting. Although I can't recall the police ever coming to the front door, as a matter of fact, the police were never called. (No one ever called the police for help—can you believe that?)

One of my sisters had to intervene time and time again. It was very painful to see my mother working two jobs and a prominent man of the community and the church deacon go at it week after week. I was glad when I could go away on the weekends and escape it all. The violent Sunday nights added another stressor to my problems. I still had to go to school on Mondays and learning was another hard issue with which I had to deal. Mother had to work two jobs so she did not have time to visit the school or check our homework. We were taught if the school calls, that we would have a restless night. Besides, most of the teachers lived in the neighborhood we grew up in, the local grocery store was where teachers held the local PTA, so much so, that I was excited to go to the store for my parents, this way they would not have to hear that I was failing in class. I always sat in the back of the class and learned to memorize what was being taught. I hardly processed any subjects especially math, spelling, and science. They were the most difficult, as there were too many rules for deciphering and evaluating to learn. I was a struggling student most of my childhood. Actually, I cooked and cleaned our house at a very young age, this way it took some of the pressure off of me when it came to school challenges. The more I did at home the less attention would be focused on my academics.

I became a master at cleaning our home and learning (life) survival techniques from watching love stories and great adventure movies on T.V. Back in the day, teachers did not refer children to the principal's office for suspension; instead, they took care of problematic behaviors in the classroom. Therefore, I did not dare get in too much trouble while in school.

My mother's weekly public address, felt like a Sunday sermon. "I will not come and get you out of jail, I will not take care of your children, you are not going to sleep all day, you will go to work, you will go to school, and you will keep my house clean." Most of us did everything she requested, with the exception of my brother. He seemed to get into a little more trouble than the others did. Had it not been for my brother taking some of the pressure off of me, I would have not endured life at home. Anger and rebellion were becoming my closest friends. I couldn't wait to grow up and leave home. I was tired of cooking and cleaning for my family. I wasn't the wife. I wanted to have fun like the others, or was this how the story goes in cinder—Deborah fairy tale. Deac called me belly friend, because I was the one who got special attention and special privileges, like sipping coffee from the small dish under his coffee cup. I felt like a rag doll when he was around me.

I did not know what was worse, going away from home or coming home. I struggled to understand the meaning of it all. I still looked forward to my weekends away even if I was uncomfortable. I didn't understand what was behind these feelings, so much was unclear to me; however, there were some things very clear to me. I cried on the way home and was nervous when I had to leave from my weekend stay away. Uncertain of what I was feeling, regardless of the environment I was in, I was in emotional pain. The excitement of going to my godmother's felt exciting, yet I knew, somehow I did not want to be there for fear that I would have to give it up. I would have to allow my feminine sexuality to be exploited. Still I want to go away; anything was better than being a slave girl who cooked and cleaned the entire weekend and then had a ringside seat to Sunday's fighting bout. We would always manage to arrive home just before the big show and it went on this way for years; peace and unrest, as both of my worlds were missing a link that never connected as my self-esteem and self-worth were depreciating at an accelerated pace.

In other words, I was having a hard time with life, I did not know if I was coming or going literally. I was at my wits end. There was no one to confide in and my mother was so consumed in working and fighting that she did not have time to notice that I was struggling. Maybe I was the scapegoat for the family. My older brother worked at the store, and my older sisters went to work with my mother sometimes. So this left me to baby sit my younger brothers and be the caretaker for our home. How could I study with all these responsibilities? Moreover, what about the emotional pain, I wanted to ask my family "what about my pain!

For example, remember the excruciating pain that goes along with a paper cut, put a band-aid on it, go prepare your favorite meal, forgetting about the wound and manage to get salt inside of it. If you are anything like me, you felt as if the wound was deeper than before you got it. Every time I get a paper cut, the same thought crosses my mind, "How could something so small, have so much pain?" Still we keep on using paper and salt, so it is with pain that we keep on carrying the memory until it becomes a lifestyle, regardless of the pain associated with it. Some of my wounds were cut so deep, they seated into my heart, mind and soul, and they resisted the Word of God.

It's not easy facing the difficult things in one's past, neither is it comfortable to confront the evils of man, at the same time, awakening dormant memories in order to put them behind you. It takes courage to attempt something again, that has hurt you more than once. Yet, for many including myself, enjoy the taste of salt and require paper to function in this life.

That's how it is with our emotions of fear, rejection, pride, control, anger, blame, and bitterness. Many of us use these self-defending emotions to keep others out or to prevent pain from seeping into our lives again. We use these addictive emotions in order to function yet we want life to stop hurting at the same time. Our life and world becomes unstable and uncertain as we keep the ones that love us out, and the people that keep hurting us are still here. Life ends in a cycle of destructive behaviors and rebellion, as our past pain teaches invaluable lessons on self-pity, shame and selfishness as we go through life unaware of our purpose in God.

LET IT OUT

My behaviors did not occur overnight, they grew out of years of not being noticed by my mother and grew until they were awakened by silent memories; pain comes over a period of time. Just like that paper cut, we are quick to cover it up and go about our cares, failing to heal our hurts. We just forget about them. Imagine a small crystal of salt seeping inside of that paper cut and instantly a reminder of the cut is awakened. We search our memory for the origin of the cut. When we are unable to remember how we cut ourselves, we react to the pain with all kinds of emotions that have nothing to do with the situation in which we live. We just know it is painful and whoever is in the crossfire gets the misdirected anger.

As such, it is with the pains of life that when something or someone triggers dormant pain, the rush of memories that overwhelms the mind and emotions will cause you to experience the suffering all over again. Suddenly, a reactive-emotional cry screams out, calling on anger and rebellion for help. If you are like me, rebellion is the first one to pick up the call. It hastily races to aid me in my pain and most of the time it shows up without thinking things through. Without being invited, pain, rebellion and their other friends come to help.

Friends like, emotional fears, making the pain larger than what it really is. Rejection, which keeps loved ones, friends and foes at a distance; prevents anyone from getting in and leaves an invisible sign on the heart that reads, *"Keep out, my heart has been broken."* Pride will show up to prevent you from seeking out help, which is needed. Control has to have everything its way, because compromising definitely is not an option when you are angry; because anger and rage have no boundaries when you are hurting. Impulsiveness reacts to the pain, as it flies off the handle emotionally. Blame will never admit "a mistake" if it does, you will never know because pride will not let him tell you and bitterness will never know how sweet life is, because of guilt and regret. They all know that if you ever taste and see how forgiving and good the Lord is, you just may want to live in the freedom of God's unconditional love.

The only way to have true freedom is to know Jesus
and that truth is the need for pure love. God is love. Let us
love one another, because love comes from God. Whoever

loves is a child of God and knows God. Whoever does not love does not know God, for God is love and God showed his love for us by sending his only son in to the world, so that we might have life through him. This is what love is: it is not that we have loved God, but that he loved us and sent his Son to be mean by which our sins are forgiven.

God is love and love is made perfect in us in order that we may have courage on the Judgment Day; and we will have it because our life in this world is the same as Christ's. There is no fear in love; perfect love drives out all fear. So then, love has not been made perfect in anyone who is afraid, because fear has to do with punishment. We love because God first loved us. (1 John 4:7-10, 16b-19 GNT)

If you never embrace your pain, you may never feel God's love. God designed each one of us with a perfect body. He not only wants us to feel His love, but to live in peace on earth in His love. There is an alternative to alleviate painful experiences from our lives so we can heal and discover the Truth behind the issue. The alternative is to have courage to face your pain, so that with the help of Jesus, you can drive out fears. The power of God is within us and therefore we are not alone, we have a loving Father who cares for us. And it is through His perfect love that we are able to become whole and break negative patterns from our past that hold us back from the healing power of God's love.

Chapter 4

Unmet Needs and the Past

"Perfect love casteth out fear: Because fear hath torment."

1 John 4:18 KJV

UNMET NEEDS AND THE PAST

Healing past hurts is a process and we can put our past behind us with the help of others and God. Sounds simple, and yet many of us have difficulty with understanding the methods of dealing with issues of our past. According to Dr. Les Carter in his book, *Putting the Past Behind; Biblical solutions to your unmet need,* the most basic need of all is the need for love. In the first moments of life, an infant cries out for someone to cradle him. We know that this craving for love is not learned or acquired because of the instinctive manner in which it is communicated. A child can detect when a parent has or has not properly responded to this need, and he can show by his reactions that he appreciates love once it is given.

This desire for love does not end when individuals mature into the later stages of life. Though each passing stage is distinguished by its own demands and tendencies, the need for love remains constant, it is this need that prompts teenagers to be particularly sensitive to the opinions of their peers. It prompts young adults to desire a mate. It prompts parents to care about the activities of their children. It prompts us all to wince when we are rebuked or to smile when we are warmly embraced. Our need for love is evident in our sexual yearnings, in our wish to be affirmed, in our preference for pleasant conversation, and in our demand for respect. Not an hour can go by without each person's expression in some reaction, thought, or emotion, the desire to be loved.

When love is constant, our behavior is stable. We become more responsible and have the ability to communicate our needs to others. Man was created to be God's handiwork (Ephesians 2: 10). Therefore, we are spirit, with a soul, living in a body. This gives each one of us the ability to focus our minds towards a higher spiritual level, the consciousness of God, which makes us a better human being, who is able to give and receive unconditional love from another. This makes our search for love almost impossible in a fallen world. Jesus' Ministry focuses on what we humans have searched for since the fall: Love. God is love. Man was created in His image. Therefore, we are love. Moreover, it is this love, which will heal, deliver and set us free. It is this love that will drive out mental illness. It is this love that will restore families. It is this love that will cause older women to teach younger women to love their husbands and children. It is this love that will transform a child's behavior. It is this love that that will bring the world back to a place of balance and peace. It is this love that mankind seeks to restore; that which we lost. Nevertheless, this love will not come without a price. This love has been given to us as a gift and when we come to know it we come in communion with the truth about love and when we lose the power to love, it becomes our individual responsibility to recovery the spirit of unconditional love.

Many will have to reflect further than others do. For only Jesus can stand in the middle to fill the basic need of love and heal hurts. Nevertheless, all have a behavior and struggle with an issue of constantly knowing love and truthfully, many search secretly for the missing link called unconditional love, as their soul hungers to heal past hurts and have answers to questions never asked. Regardless if it's physical, emotional or spiritual, we as a people hunger for unconditional love.

THE REASON BEHIND CAIN'S ANGER AND A LESSON ABOUT REJECTION

By the Lord's help I have gotten a son and she named him Cain. Later she gave birth to another son, Abel. Abel became a shepherd, but Cain was a farmer. After some time Cain brought some of his harvest and gave it as an offering to the Lord. Then Abel brought the first lamb born to one of his sheep, killed it, and gave the best parts of it as an offering. The Lord was pleased with Abel and his offering, but he rejected Cain and his offering. Cain became furious, and he scowled in anger. Then the Lord said to Cain, Why are you angry? Why that scowl on your face? If you had done the right thing, you would be smiling; but because you have done evil, sin is crouching at your door. It wants to rule you, but you must overcome it. Then Cain said to his brother Abel, Let's go out in the fields. When they were out in the fields, Cain turned on his brother and killed him. The Lord asked Cain, Where is your brother Abel? He answered, I don't know. Am I supposed to take care of my brother? Then the Lord said, why have you done this terrible thing? (Genesis 4: 1-10 GNT)

The birth of a child is awesome for some couples. It's a time when a mother and father both are able to share in their mutual love as they give birth to the newest member of their family. While this is an exciting time for the parents, it can be a serious problem, over time for the other children in the family. Particularly, if the parents fail to ensure that their other children are emotionally welcoming the birthing experience.

It appears that Cain was tested by God concerning the subject of rejection and it's apparent that he did not do well on this test. There were many negative consequences to Cain's inability to handle rejection, anger, and a temperament that was explosive. The story suggests that God Himself warned Cain well in advance, regarding his attitude, facial expressions and secrets within his heart. *Anger* stood in the middle of receiving *God's warning* to deal with a bigger problem. Consequently, Cain failed to heed God's explanation, as anger was blocking his hearing receptors. His anger problem did not just happen. It developed over time, progressing to uncontrollable rage causing extensive grief for him and his parents.

When parents fail to understand a child's temperament or emotional needs, this permits the advancement of, and opens the door for, unwanted behaviors in our children. Negative behaviors and unmet emotional needs will likely worsen causing frustration and discouragement to both parents and child, particularly, behaviors of anger and resentment towards other siblings. This is especially true if they are dethroning the eldest child from their parents' spotlight! Dethroning can take on different meanings to different children, simply stated they have been replaced or removed from a position of power. For example, a new school, a single parent dating, a new group home or foster home/parents or relocating (even if it is two miles away from their previous home). Today's generation is longing for consistency and emotional support which is essential to diminish unwanted behaviors.

A child who is crying out for help and emotional support may use anger to get their parents' attention to meet their needs. There are many reasons why children behave in the manner which they do. Children with learned behaviors, environmental concerns and blemished genetics (DNA) have their own motives for seeking out attention. Many times their words cannot express their needs or the child has not learned how to articulate clearly. To this day many adults say one thing and do another and relationships suffer because of failure to communicate clearly, and the inability to express feeling or understand what is being said. Their body language does not match the words being expressed. It's like working on a complex cross word puzzle without a dictionary.

Children have many complexities and there are times when only by divine intervention will the Spirit reveal to us the cause of an apparent social breakdown syndrome. Many young children cannot describe their unmet needs in words; therefore, their only means of communication is to act out their pain through behaviors. Many times as parents/guardians, we are unable to discern between our child's emotional needs and behaviors because of our own set of issues. In the case with my grandson, Adrian, he was crying out for help, and because his parents were deaf, he only knew acting out. This is my story. In no way am I saying that all children act out. What I am saying is, to thine own self be true, and look beneath the surface of a child's pain. If this is left unattended for long periods of time, the result could be fatal. (Hopefully, you were not mirroring me, replacing emotional support with comfort, convenience, financial and material possession).

Maybe rejection was carved in Cain from the onset. It appears to be a mystery. What one can surmise is that he used his time doing duty, seeking to fulfill a void for attention for which he so emotionally yearned. This is common for today's generation, as it was for me. A child is born into the family and the newborn seems to get all the attention, then you waste years fighting for a position to be loved and nurtured.

As my hypothetical mind challenged me to think outside of the box, is it possible that his mother (Eve), simply ignored or was so busy with her own issues of unresolved blame and guilt within her marriage, which she failed to focus or deal with her son's anger problem? Was it possible that her oldest son's unpleasant behaviors of anger were unnoticed and went unchecked by Adam?—After all he was mandated to work long hours in the thorny fields. Adam's grounds were cursed, so he had to work extremely hard, which caused weariness and frustration as well. It seems like the entire workings of the family nucleus was struggling through emotional roadblocks; and so it is for many of God's people today

If we are to have any form of *hope*, this generation must prepare to spiritually and physically battle for our children's souls, minds, wills and emotions. It may require this generation to take a stand, attempting to unravel ancestral sins and emotions which are connected to rejection, guilt and shame. God has marked each of us for an expected end. *He is all knowing* and His ways are too high for any of us to understand. Nevertheless, what we can understand is that the same unblemished blood that was used then to redeem Cain is available today.

God in His tender mercy did not take blood for blood, because He had a better plan. I believe he allowed Cain to suffer, survive and build a city, in which his descendents would have an opportunity to change generations and in the process receive healing and blessings for many generations to come. Cain's pain and *isolation process* allotted him time to re-evaluate his life, established a city for God and receive a promise in the midst of his struggles; however, the cycle continued.

Adam and Even were given a second chance as well and the result was a son, Seth. Hidden between blame, shame, death and pain is forgiveness, healing, and blessings. The healing and promise were the results of a second chance and a generation who changed their ways and called upon the name of the Lord for help in times of difficulty. Enoch was transformed at 65 years old and his ways (behaviors) pleased God. In the midst of their intimate time together, God was so pleased with his life that He walked him to heaven.

Sometimes there are generations who appear to have lost it. Consider Noah, who according to his neighbors and friends, was out of his mind. While they were having fun and morally corrupt, Noah silently, but openly obeyed the *voice of God*. He demonstrated his obedience by building an ark in the midst of a dry land. He was ridiculed about doing such an outlandish thing, but despite being laughed at, he obeyed God. His expected end (future) was the promise of safety. He endured harsh living conditions. His environment was *extremely – unsanitary*, nonetheless, in the process of time he and his family received God's promise. Just like many of us, there are extreme conditions in our lives and for many of us there are struggles within our families, but this is not the time to give up. I know! Hold on, your promise is on the way.

THE STRUGGLE

In the year 2000, or even in the year 2005, if someone were to ask me a question regarding my life or life experiences or experiences *they felt I should share with others,* I was smart enough to avoid answering them and smoothly changed the subject in order to relieve myself from a tedious and embarrassing past. It was a tedious task, but it was simple. I was good at changing topics about my personal experiences. I was not about to look back, turnaround or even face a life that was filled with personal struggles and emotional pain.

Now that I have matured in God, looking back is the only way I could move forward. Nestled between feelings as if God had abandoned me, feeling unloved, ashamed and rejected by closing the door on the past is my final attempt to unravel a life filled with pain and bitterness. Especially, from a past that I cannot change! My past is a part of me. Now I look at it more like a time in history. It is now written in the history books. I lived feeling as if my struggles were unique, but the more I reached out to others, I realized that our lives shared the same "tormenting pain."

You see, I was teased all the time around the holidays and to this day, it's a task to celebrate my birthday with family and friends. "Don't you all remember the time when we only got a red ball and *her* for Christmas" or "I didn't name you the nurse in the hospital asked me if she could; she saw your dark hair and big eyes and fell in love with you!" These painful messages sent emotional signals that stopped me from experiencing joy and fulfillment of a wanted birth. These simple words were funny to everyone, it was a joke, but it was not funny for me at the time. Maybe my family was not aware that words can hurt even the youngest of minds.

My siblings made me feel as if it was my fault that they did not receive presents year after year. I was the fifth child of a single parent and when my mother would tell me this story, it saddened me, leaving me feeling unwanted and often times angry with her. Eventually, these words grew in my heart, causing me to never truly bond with her. For clinical reasons this is an *'attachment wound'*. For me there was only one-way to control my pain and that was to seek out emotional ties that were unhealthy and cycled destructive relationships. I suffered silently and lonely for a very long time.

There was a deep black hole within my heart and I never knew or understood why. There were many unanswered questions that I longed to have answered. How could they not notice what was going on with me? Was it my fault? Why did bad things happen to me? Maybe if others knew that sexual images were carved within my memory they would understand my behaviors. Thinking to myself, I said, why didn't my mother notice the pain her child was experiencing, or help me to overcome the negative effects? Maybe we were extremely disconnected which prevented us from connecting in the spirit realm.

On the other hand, what I do remember is that I was young and innocent at one point in my life. In addition, over time, I learned to accept unwanted touches as love. As I grew older, I was disciplined for seeking out these unnatural responses to an unmet need- love. Sexual abuse is not new or unique- *'For there is nothing new under the sun'*. Maybe it is the season that families reach out to love ones and help those in need of unconditional love and forgiveness of self and others. The consequences are far greater, when left untreated, internal torment has a way to fester into bitterness and secret shame.

TAMAR'S SECRET

Amnon had a good friend, Jonadab, the son of David's brother Shimeah. Jonadab was exceptionally streetwise. He said to Amnon, "Why are you moping around like this, day after day—you, the son of the king! Tell me what's eating at you." "In a word, Tamar," said Amnon. "My brother Absalom's sister. I'm in love with her." "Here's what you do," said Jonadab. "Go to bed and pretend you're sick. When your father comes to visit you, say, "Have my sister Tamar come and prepare some supper for me here where I can watch her and she can feed me."' So Amnon took to his bed and acted sick. When the king came to visit, Amnon said, "Would you do me a favor? Have my sister Tamar come and make some nourishing dumplings here where I can watch her and be fed by her."David sent word to Tamar who was home at the time: "Go to the house of your brother Amnon and prepare a meal for him."

So Tamar went to her brother Amnon's house. She took dough, kneaded it, formed it into dumplings, and cooked them while he watched from his bed. But when she took the cooking pot and served him, he wouldn't eat. Amnon said, "Clear everyone out of the house," and they all cleared out. Then he said to Tamar, "Bring the food into my bedroom, where we can eat in privacy." She took the nourishing dumplings she had prepared and brought them to her brother Amnon in his bedroom. But when she got ready to feed him, he grabbed her and said, "Come to bed with me, sister!"

"No, brother!" she said, "Don't hurt me! This kind of thing isn't done in Israel! Don't do this terrible thing! Where could I ever show my face? And you—you'll be out on the street in disgrace. Oh, please! Speak to the king— he'll let you marry me." But he wouldn't listen. Being much stronger than she, he raped her. No sooner had Amnon raped her than he hated her—an immense hatred. The hatred that he felt for her was greater than the love he'd had for her. "Get up," he said, "and get out!"

"Oh no, brother," she said. "Please! This is an even worse evil than what you just did to me!" But he wouldn't listen to her. He called for his valet. "Get rid of this woman. Get her out of my sight! And lock the door after

her." The valet threw her out and locked the door behind her. She was wearing a long-sleeved gown. (That's how virgin princesses used to dress from early adolescence on.) Tamar poured ashes on her head, then she ripped the long-sleeved gown, held her head in her hands, and walked away, sobbing as she went. Her brother Absalom said to her, "Has your brother Amnon had his way with you? Now, my dear sister, let's keep it quiet—a family matter. He is, after all, your brother. Don't take this so hard." Tamar lived in her brother Absalom's home, bitter and desolate.

(2 Samuel 13:3-20 Message)

Unlike Tamar, my brother was not my life coach and I was void of maternal guidance. For fear that my mother would be ashamed of me or if she would believe my story. I struggled on both ends. On one end the person whom I trusted was telling me how much they loved me and not to tell anyone and on the other end, I was unable to share my tormenting experiences with a praying mother because I feared her.

The one I trusted and longed to be with did not tell me the truth. Now I know how it feels when it's the family who wants to keep the secrets. Most of my ills were tied to my bloodline. I heard adults say they would go to their grave with these types of stories so they would not bring disgrace on family members. Could anyone care less about the tormenting power of bitterness rendering the victim helpless or was protecting family pride more important than the truth?

THE PERILS OF SUNDAY'S DERAILMENT

My parents argued almost every Sunday night. As I recall, there were many reasons for them to have these disputes; Sunday's derailments were a way of life. On top of their own issues, there were several children and one of us either stole money, failed to clean the dishes, came home late, or whatever my parents forgot to take care of that week. They had a way to clear out old business before the new week started; unless they forgot to discipline us, then next week would be double the trouble. We were reminded often of the consequences if we were not honest. Their method of discipline was all about **tough love** and a Godly future.

My memory recalls my brother being a recipient of *'tough love'* and the effects of this tough love lingers an emotional aroma over him to this day and he speaks about it as if it was yesterday. One day during his weekly sermon of tough love, tears escaped his eyes. He managed to turn his body and laugh as if it was a joke from a comedy show. He often used the metaphor, "I used to be tied like a pig, but if it had not been for those beatings, I would not be like I am today." I never could understand his rationale, seeing that addictions were constantly knocking on his front door. His relationships with his children were challenged or broken. Even his dreams of becoming a professional ball player were hindered by the fear of being beaten during a time when it was deemed socially appropriate to induce fear in a child.

It has been well over forty years since I witnessed my brother tied with a rope and beaten naked. Back in the day, parents called discipline—beating the "hell out of you!" As I reflect over my life, who in their 'right mind' wanted to be a part of this model praying family. I write this not wanting to hurt, but with permission to heal and mend a broken past and to tell others especially within a hurting society, that they are not alone in their plight to freedom. As they too can breakdown these secrets walls of guilt and shame especially when one considers that guilt and shame are universal landmarks created by the enemy to keep us from unleashing our faith and trusting a loving God.

Webster defines shame as a painful emotion caused by consciousness of guilt, a condition of humiliating disgrace or disrepute; something that brings strong regret, censure, or reproach; a cause of feeling shame.

I'm told that living in prison can have a devastating effect on you, particularly; if one has never emotionally experienced the massiveness of freedom that salvation offers your heart, soul and society. These simple but painful reflections only remind me that none of us are truly free from the torments of our past. How can one still not be free in the midst of freedom? Unfortunately, when my mother became ill and resigned to the hands of Leukemia, we all were challenged to discover that this truth did not come with an easy answer. We all struggled with our emotions and prayed that a loving Savior would keep us together.

"For nothing is secret that shall not be made manifest; neither anything hid."

All this hurt, pain and guilt were manifested into negative behaviors towards self, God and others. Until one day in the midst of one of the loneliest times of my life, I found the love of Jesus, who pardoned my sins and taught me how to forgive and release those who shared in my physical, emotional and spiritual pain. Yes, a loving Savior stood up and covered me with His blood in the midst of all my pain, anger, hate, bitterness, control and fear. In the midst of all my suffering, Jesus met me with his unconditional love, bidding me to come and find rest in Him.

Chapter 5

The Struggles of Parents – Not Forsaken

"I will be your father, and you will be my sons and daughters, says the Lord All-Powerful."

2 Corinthians 6:18 ICB

My son, if you will take my words to your heart, storing up my laws in your mind; So that your ear gives attention to wisdom, and your heart is turned to knowledge; Truly, if you are crying out for good sense, and your request is for knowledge; If you are looking for her as for silver, and searching for her as for stored-up wealth; Then the fear of the Lord will be clear to you, and knowledge of God will be yours. For the Lord gives wisdom; out of his mouth come knowledge and reason: He has salvation stored up for the upright, he is a breastplate to those in whom there is no evil; He keeps watch on the ways which are right, and takes care of those who have the fear of him. Then you will have knowledge of righteousness and right acting, and upright behavior, even of every good way. For wisdom will come into your heart, and knowledge will be pleasing to your soul; Wise purposes will be watching over you, and knowledge will keep you; Giving you salvation from the evil man, from those whose words are false;

(Proverbs 2:1-12 BBE)

THE STRUGGLES OF PARENTS – NOT FORSAKEN

In spite of all the heartaches, struggles, and painful experiences that have engulfed my life, there is still a sense of victory that lives deep within my soul. I am a survivor and for that, I give God all the Glory for the knowledge of the true meaning of salvation. As I acknowledge Him for all my victories and for allowing me to care for a generation that shares similar struggles.

I remember listening in silence to elders and watching my favorite television family shows. I was going to love and provide for my children regardless of the negative circumstances that surrounded their conception. There was one thing I always knew, my children were not going to endure suffering as I did. Everything that was possible for a single parent to do, I did, but somehow, I never felt as if it was enough. Questioning their safety became an obsession. There were many parenting skills that went uncheck. The school of *hard knocks* taught what was required. I remember my mother instructing all of us to take care of our own children, work hard and be strong regardless of the adversities you may face.

As I pray for Godly wisdom, knowledge, and understanding for the requirements of raising children who are challenged emotionally, as well as understanding a loving and forgiving God. In order to spiritually parent a challenged and creative generation, it is my desire to know God, both as mother and father in order for Him to teach me His thoughts and reveal His plans for my life, in a generation surrounded by toxic influences of historical sins.

In order for me to change unwanted behaviors that have been carved within my memory, my first order of business was to have God's Word written in my heart. It's evident that some parenting styles must be challenged even changed, if we want our children to survive in an ever so changing society. We did!

Today's children have to learn how to fight spiritually, because of the battle within their soul; however we have enlisted many of them in a boot camp that has nurtured them with anger, hostility, and distorted love. Some of today's young mothers have challenged parenting styles. As a result, children are taken away or they are mandated by the courts to seek a parenting course to teach the basics to meet their child's needs and/or change their parenting methods.

According to Drs. Ann B. and Richard J. Barnet, MD, in their book, *The Youngest Minds, Parenting and Genes in the Development of Intellect and Emotion:*

> *Discussions about the meaning of childhood, the special requirements of children, and the role of parents generate heated disagreement about the most basic questions; what do children need in order to develop into normal, happy, and caring adults? When do they need it? Who should provide it? The answers have changed over the course of history in response to differing cultural and economic forces, and, more recently, also as a result of the research of child psychologists and other scientist.*
>
> *In traditional cultures, mothers normally learn their care giving routines from their own mothers or some other older woman and believe that they are caring for their baby in the best or the only way. Modern women, however, may instantly change their ways under the influence of outside authorities and in the light of new knowledge or circumstance.*

If the mother is physically or emotionally unavailable, or the child fears that he will be abandoned, he becomes chronically anxious. If the primary caregiver is remote, depressed, uncaring, or inconsistent and unreliable, or if the people who fill that role come and go with great frequency, the resulting distortions of the primary relationship.... can lead to difficulties in forming deep relationships with others in adult life.

Separation anxiety is what a child will experience if taken away from his parent too early in the relationship. When a child knows that his or her parent is returning they are able to build a secure attachment as an infant. Their life is somewhat predictable. On the other hand, when a child goes from place to place, constantly moving from home to home, their life is disrupted. The same is the case with schooling; they fail to have confidence in the adults who care for them. These children grow up to be suspicious, angry, filled with rage and violent, lacking trust in the very one who is to care for them.

This was the life of Adrian, my grandson. A life filled with transitions, I guess he must have attended six schools before the age of eight and moved about four times before he was three-years-old. He hardly had time to bond with anyone at such a young age. On top of that, I interrupted his life by keeping him throughout the summer months, long weekends and holidays. What a disconnect in his life.

LIFE IS FILLED WITH CHANGES

Our life is in a constant state of transition, where babies grow up to be children, children adolescents, adolescent teenagers, a teen a young adult, young adults, an adult a senior, a senior transitions to death, and death becomes new life. However, there are some us who are stuck in a period of time, a time where they are never able to experience the fullness of their life on earth. The realities are such, that in order to experience true joy, you have to learn where your painful experiences originated so you understand how to change, heal and live in a future ordained by God. I don't agree with everything in his book, but deep within this little book were a few golden nuggets that challenged my thoughts.

Dr. Alberto Villoldo, writes in, *Mending the Past and Healing the Future with Soul Retrieval:*

> *Our destiny is not the same as our future: while the future is what will happen later, destiny is in every instant, and we can always make ourselves available to it. Destiny is saying yes to the calling we're born with, while fate is what happens when we fight or ignore our calling... We dull our lives by explaining them away with a list of causes that lie beyond our control.*

How one mends the past, determines the course of their destiny. Hope and healing is possible, but it may require some of us to go back in time. Yes, it maybe a painful and emotional experience, but it seems that both are required in healing brokenness.

There are some facts in one's life that cannot be changed. You may want to reason many of these historical truths, point the blame to others, or even block these ills from your life, but the truth is, *history is a part of life!* In order to live again, there will be times that you will just have to take the time to put the pieces back in the right order. All of us were born to live out our destiny with great expectation. A destiny uniquely designed by a wise God, regardless of roadblocks, barriers and negative influences, which have encapsulated us to think otherwise.

Chapter 6

Discerning Fear

"Love is like a mirror. When you love another you become his mirror and he becomes yours... And reflecting each other's love you see infinity."

Leo Buscalglia

DISCERNING FEAR

Deep down within I love my grandson, yet he was afraid of me and I did not like him at the time. He was making my life miserable. My husband was working at night and I had to be alone and deal with Adrian's behaviors. It seemed like at night alone with him he would get emotionally out of control. Over time, Adrian and I were learning to self-regulate and manage our fears. I feared his safety and he feared I would leave him. Besides, he didn't trust me, despite being family. There were days when I noticed him jumping at the mere sight of a lizard on the porch, while I was watching him outside playing. Yelling and screaming when one would run into the flowers or by his feet. I caught myself yelling at him for yelling. It felt like I was his mirror. He was the one with an overwhelming sense of anger and fear. I grew obsessed and determined to discover the truth behind his pain, not to mention an enormous amount of guilt that over shadowed me.

There were many layers of pain beneath his fears and anger and we were only looking at his surface behaviors, as they blocked our view from the truth. His behaviors just got in the way and each time they did we reacted as if it was the first time they visited our family. The shouting, tantrums, and bullying were acted out weekly. In the bathroom, kitchen, parties, and weddings or in the car, his disruptive behaviors would occur anywhere and at any given moment. They were unpredictable behaviors.

One day out of nowhere, I was acting like him or worse. I was in his world and it was clear that neither of us were in control of our emotions. It seemed like what I wanted for him was not happening fast enough. What I wanted was a "normal child." A child that would follow directions, play with other children and not have any problems for me to deal with. I wanted a robot and I wanted my old life back! Whatever that was, I wanted it.

How could this be happening to me again! Especially at a time when I was just learning how to live in peace. Before this all I knew was peace, even if it was short lived. I longed for the day my parenting would be over, but somehow it felt like it never ended. Familiar spirits were lurking and I was yelling and using the same words as old. "You will honor me! You will respect me! I am the adult here!" I used these trusty words just to regain my power and position. I was using my authority as an adult to take-over a hostile situation and I was ready with bible verses just in case the enemy was lurking his ugly head. I wanted to be in control.

Even if I knew his temperament was a compulsive in control, I was too close to the situation to do what was right. I was right in my own eyesight, establishing my own righteousness in my home. How *dogmatic* was I in my thinking! The both of us were breaking rules and violating God's command regarding our relationship. I had yet to understand why I was being pulled into his world of fight and fear. It seemed as if my emotions were not my own.

The term *"Emotional hijack"* is used to describe an explosive and uncontrollable rage, fear, or excitement that overwhelms rational appraisal and judgment in most people at some time and in some people too much of the time.[1] Negative emotions, guilt, and regret were knocking at the door of my heart. Again, I was being attacked by an overwhelming amount of guilt and shame. In the midst of trying to find peace and a moment to meditate in the presence of God, all these feelings were coming at me like a flood. The Spirit of God spoke gently to me, "Stop allowing others to rule in my place of peace."

My guilt was maternal, as my fear was laced with deceit! My motherly instinct was telling me that this child longed to be with his maternal mother. In the same fashion, despite how he was feeling, I was still struggling with my mother leaving me with someone else. Beyond that, I was struggling emotionally with both my mother's and youngest daughter's love. Four generations genetically exposed to guilt, rejection, fear, and unstable emotions. How could this be? Was it in my bloodline that was preventing us from living a whole life? I refused to believe that God intended for us to live like this, guilty and bound to fear. This was not God's plan for my family and definitely not the plan of salvation. Freedom! Several months later, while we were having dinner, he said to me, "grandma maybe returning home to my mother- would be an impossible dream, but I still should have hope and be positive."

"Sometimes it takes a painful experience to make us change our ways."

Proverbs 20:30 GNT

IN THE BLOOD

One day I wanted to have a "pow-wow" peace treaty with my daughter. After months of broken trust, I finally had the courage to sit down with her and discuss our relationship. From a distance, you could see the smoke rising from her. She was very upset. One thought was replaying in my head, "Overlook the lie and look at the child through the eyes of Christ, with unconditional love." It was time to heal all this pain between the two of us and it was time to tear down the walls of pain, mistrust and fear.

Feeling very nervous, we sat down together on the bed. I asked her with a newfound sincere love in my tone and body expression; "What's going on, it seems like you and I never have bonded like a mother and daughter should for all these years?" Her words ripped through my heart, as tears streamed down her face, *"I thought you didn't want me. You made me live with Nana all by myself."*

"Wow!" I said to her as my heart dropped to the floor. Her words weighed me down with even more distress and guilt. All these years she held in her the thought of her mother not wanting her. I wanted to give her a dissertation of my life, but this was not the time to explain my reasons for leaving her with her grandmother. My arms reached out so natural, only desiring to relieve her from her pain. As I was holding her close to my heart, wiping her tears away, I too began to cry and share emotionally in her pain.

Now, I understand her difficulties and her inability to understand the logic behind her having to stay with my mother. My daughter was too young to understand the reasons of living with a grandmother so far away from her mother. She was only a child and her mind was not developed enough to understand the complexities of my life.

As I embraced her, I knew I did not have her heart. I was only feeling her pain. She was still angry and rebelling from my decision to take control of my future. Holding her did not set things right. Her heart was hardened from feelings of rejection and unmet needs of a mother's love. It would take time to heal the both of us, particularly our emotions.

Unfortunately, it was a few weeks later she moved out of our home. Regardless she was my daughter and I would be waiting for her return with loving-open arms. I felt like my prodigal daughter would eventually exhaust and return home safely. I waited and watched for her return and home is where she returned. It was the longest nine months of my life, but there was even more emotions added to her previously unresolved hurts and unmet needs.

Still, it was a joy to see her and we celebrated her return, it was time to mend the past and live, laugh and love this time more peacefully. I was determined our relationship would take on a different tone and that unconditional love would rule my heart, in order to ease her pain. I knew we both had more compassion in our hearts.

Miracles don't grow on trees they grow in the heart.

Small changes were noticeable over dinner and social events; she was finally coming to join us. Although she wasn't talking to any of us, she was coming to join us for dinner. I didn't mind the process. Coming out of her room was a sign of hope, because *with God all things are possible.* If things were going to change in our family, we all had emotional work, as faith without works is dead.

First, we decided to increase our prayer life and family devotion time. Then we had to make a commitment as a family to change our hearts towards one another. Finally, we had to make an intentional decision to defuse stressful situations in our home and those around us. Stress was having devastating effects on us and we were making adjustments since adding a new member (my grandson) to our home. Besides, he was enough to keep all of us on edge; he was a handful! I kept thinking, since there are three adults in the home, how could one adult *manage him alone*?

I soon realized my oldest wasn't coming home in the usual manner; and I couldn't help notice how she had resigned to stress. It had taken its toll. Stress had written its name on her face. She no longer smiled, she was irritable, and her friends were now her safe haven. Her ability to concentrate on her career and academics were diminishing and she removed her son from our unhealthy environment. Beyond that, she couldn't handle the emotional challenges in the one she loved, as if it was her own beloved son.

Adrian's emotional challenges were severe enough to interfere with his daily functioning, understanding boundaries and his ability to respond with enough verbal intelligence to those who were seeking answers regarding his past life. Nevertheless, there was a connection between emotions, stress, and fear. They all were robbing my family's ability to love him unconditionally. I had no idea of the severity of his emotional needs, unwanted behaviors, and the effects it had on his development. Negative behaviors resulting from domestic violence, learning problems, and uncertainty of his future, were carved in his memory and over time, it caused his heart to harden toward those who were now caring for him.

Drs. Ann B. and Richard J. Barnet, MD, authors of *The Youngest Minds*, explain that an emotion may be initiated in any one of many body systems, triggered by an external event or some internal trigger such as a pain or a memory. Within the brain, numerous components of emotion systems overlap, interlock, and control responses that sometimes appear similar. This makes the exact neural basis for a behavior extremely difficult to pinpoint. Stress is the normal response of the body to fearsome or painful stimuli that disturbs its equilibrium. It is managed largely by interactions among the hormones of the adrenal and pituitary glands and the hypothalamus, the "stress axis." Emotional arousal is increased and memory formation is enhanced. However, sustained stress can produce numerous pathological effects throughout the body and the brain. Stress increases the production of cortisol, a hormone secreted by the adrenal gland. Chronic excess of cortisol has been shown to accelerate the loss of certain types of neurons, including those of the hippocampus, a center vital for the formation of memories. Chronic stress adversely affects memory and learning and this may have particularly pernicious effects on children's development [2]

My life felt like a war zone, growing fearful that at anytime it would be I who would turn and betray him, as I aged and my weight increased from all the emotional stress. My mind played games with me. As signals replayed 'hurt him,' thoughts of getting even did come to my mind, and very often. *I am human not divine* and the possibility of hurting the one I loved wore on me. The relationship I felt for him was more like love-hate. On a good day-, I loved him; when he violated my rules, I was filled with hatred towards him. The atmosphere included a mixture of emotions and they all produced negative energy like anger, blame, disappointment, guilt, and resentment, especially if I had an emotional day at the office. I no longer had time to regroup and renew my mind before interacting with family. I was emotionally attacked upon entering my home; it was like pouring salt in an old wound.

In essence, it was difficult to manage his emotions and the negative emotions I was feeling towards him. He wanted total control of every situation and I was not about to let that happen without a fight. Stress had one objective and that was to consume us with emotions and that is precisely what it was doing to the both of us. He was displaying the behaviors of an adult, yet emotionally he was a five year old wanting to play games and consume most of my time with his negative behaviors. Is this call attention seeking? What was really happening to him? Or did his mother allow him too much responsibility to speak up for her (she is deaf) in public places and he thought he had the power to do the same for me. I was not having a child control me, that's for sure. So remind me of the reason behind the proverbs young mother's use, *"this is the man of my house"* or *"this is my little man!"* I was only trying to help him and he would not allow me to connect or take the place of his mother, as he reminded me daily of this fact. I only wanted the best for him and both his parents (his father is my son). Although he loved his father, his heart was with his mother. He had to prove to me that he was not going to be at peace with his new living arrangements.

Now, I felt the other side to Cain's anger-**REJECTION!** Constantly on the alert for ungodly expressions, checking for signs of sulking and disapproval, as I feared that rage would take control of my emotions in a silent moment. My heart was bleeding and broken. Feeling like a city under siege! Burdened down with guilt, my head and heart was sick from the sole of my feet to the top of my head. Nothing was stable within me. I was far from perfect, more like a ruined city; a city with walls that were built on strongholds of stress and fear. Friends and neighbors were constantly sending signals that we were doing a good job and to tell you the truth it felt more strenuous than holding two even three jobs. I know, because I did.

People were praising us for the changes they witnessed, particularly at social events and elders saw what neither of us could. We saw the trees and they saw through the trees and witnessed the forest in the midst. I only knew our private world was being turned upside down. In fact, we had enlisted to nurture a strong willed child- with an erratic temperament.

My feelings wore on me and I was unhappy about the bruises on my body. They were all a result of kicks during brief moments of anger, especially when he was disappointed, rejected or worried about what was in his future. I was uncomfortable and constantly worried if anyone noticed the blue and purple bite marks on my arms. One would always find me dressed in long shirts especially during the summer's heat. There were a few times at night, I found myself crying, praying and longing for my husband to return home from work, just so he could provide me with emotional support and acknowledge that he loved me still.

I knew that he had to work these hours, as no one knew what time the phone would ring during the day requesting that one of us come to the school. Yet, my own fears and personal "stuff" were getting in the way causing me to emotionally react to my husband. Helping my own blood was no longer rewarding but a constant struggle. Many mornings my eyelids were heavy from sleepless nights, keeping one eye open and alert, watching and praying for the sun to rise. I prayed for a better day despite learning to predict emotional outbursts and monitor triggers that provoked him. I prayed for Jesus to help me get through one more day.

The door to rejection was open, as I became its victim. Abandonment was not far behind lurking to find its place in my mind. It was a long time since these dark feelings over shadowed me, *for I never forgot what they felt like.* My oldest came home, to a typical day at the house. Her appearance was unusual as she announced that she was moving out. Her reasons simply stated, "I can no longer expose my son to this and can no longer witness him in pain". She turned and said on her way out the door, "My last day living here is the end of this month." Her words cut my heart. I never in my life expected her to leave *me* like this. Out of nowhere, she echoed behind a closing door "give him back- he's not worth it, why didn't they tell you everything about him before they gave him to us". My family was splitting apart as anger, guilt and resentment covered my mind and heart. The enemy came in the door and was doing his job- killing, stealing and destroying my family, and I allowed it.

How could I honor her request? He was part of me. He was my seed. I knew deep inside there was hope for him to feel love for me. The way he once did. Yet, I wanted freedom from it all. I didn't want to live in an abusive relationship. Even if it was a child!

It felt like an abusive relationship and my feelings were not telling me any different. Is it possible for a child to be tormented by fear?—A mirror of his environment. Distorted love is the worst kind and he was in need of his soul being healed by a divine and loving Savior. *It's with His stripes we are healed.* The bruises on my body were only symbolic to what a loving Savior endured so we could learn the truth about His love. I was merely a stand in; until I accepted truth and learned to be His mirror image. Alone, I could do nothing, but with the true Suffering Savior, there was hope.

If this child was ever going to overcome his trauma and the images engraved upon his young heart and mind, it would encompass more than a dose of medication. His pain flowed much deeper and he needed peace that flowed from the thrones of God. It took all this before the peace of God open my mind to the fact that the child longed to be with his maternal mother. It was his mother's love and protection for which he longed, and his heart was open to the enemy, as long as there was a hole. He really was no different from me, except I was an adult.

Then one night during devotion we prayed, asking the Lord to assign His angels to protect him and give him peace in his heart and mind, so he could learn to be secure in his new home. One day in his journey, he would accept love from a distant place.

Then it happened, one evening, at the dinner table, he said to me, "Grandma, you know what the boys in the group told me? If I break things and get in trouble in your house, you will get mad and send me home to my mother." As I stared into his eyes, it was one of the hardest days of my life. It was time to explain to him that *"going home was not possible, it would be awhile."* That night, I knew that one of us better do some quick adjusting and since I wanted to be the adult, then adjusting emotionally had better start with me.

> *Dr. Alberto Villoldo, Mending the Past and Healing the Future with Soul Retrieval writes; "We wonder where their stubbornness, determination, or absentmindedness came from. Certainly, we applaud exceptional athletic skills or musical talent, but we fear other extraordinary characteristics such as a high need for movement and novelty that makes it difficult to sit still in class. In today's medication- prone society, many of these children wind up getting treated with Ritalin, Prozac, and other drugs that would have numbed the creativity out of many of the geniuses of the past. We have to wonder: Are all of these really medical disorders, or could many be expressions*

of a unique calling? We continually experience and re-experience our past stories without changing their outcomes.'

ADHD is a childhood disability that interferes with a child's ability to remain focused and pay attention, or the child has a difficult time controlling his or her movement and behaviors. Some children can be in the middle of a project, hear a noise, and then become easily distracted. ADHD is a common childhood disorder; these children are artistic, talented and fearfully and wonderfully made. They too are created in God's image, yet most people look at them as lazy, and problematic. Have you stop to wonder that when these children grow up, they become adults?

I remembered my, fears as a child and that I could not share my concerns with anyone. It was time that I listened to him as I was experiencing a break in my demeanor, I too was having life challenges, disorganized, and having difficulties getting to work on time. I was restless, and my personal relationship with my husband was just seeing a sign of hope over the past year since my grandson was living in our home. I was no different than he was and it was a big relief to know that I could connect to my grandson. I just grew up and was never diagnosed with a mental disorder or ADHD. Yet, I was living in my own modern jungle, where I was trying to survive. My stubbornness was shifting.

Although, at times it felt as if we were living in a jungle, where I was constantly searching out safe havens in which my children and grandchildren could live free from the problems and ills within our society. A society filled with prejudgments, sexual abuse, drugs and alcohol, sex and pornography and the negative impacts of parental neglect and child abuse. Adding to this was the lust of money, materialism and failing marriages across the globe. The times in which we live feels like the "survival of the fittest".

Today's generation is always on the move, but it appears as if we are never moving forward. Many of us are challenged with our own stuff, often times it is difficult to understand the grief of another. A loss is a loss and pain is pain. Given that children learn from their environment, their experiences are carved into their memory. It makes one question: if a child is not responsible for their behavior then who is? It's hard to make sense out of all that's going on in today's society, for that fact, anywhere in the world. Children are learning by what they see, feel and their experiences. It is possible to understand how a child's early memory has an impact on their future. Not merely for children, but adults as well. For some of us, the past and the future both feel the same.

THE DOLLAR BILL

As I reflect on the longest summer of my life and with great disappointment, I never truly forgave my father for breaking my heart. Out of all the things he told me, I believe him when he told me I could live with him. My heart was filled with hope all year waiting for the day, which I did not have to go to my godmother's for the summer. To this day, the memories are painful. My maternal father had said earlier that school year that I could live with him during the summer months, but it never happened! It was the last day of school. I was in the fifth grade and ready to go off to live with him. I was dressed like a fairy tale princess, wearing an orange dress with long white lace flowing down the front, brown sandals with gold ornaments across the top bands and my green suitcase was packed with enough clothes to last an entire summer. I called my father in hopes that my mother could possibly drive me to his house before the sun set and darkness filled the sky.

The telephone rings were longer than usual and the longer the rings the more time to dwell on everything that could possibly be wrong, none of my thoughts were good. Worry consumed me and fear had its grips on my heart. It would be the first time in my life that I actually stayed with my father and his wife, a wife whom I had never met before. My excitement was turning into fear as tears were starting to build up in my eyes. I told my friends, that I was going to have a great summer with my father. It meant more than a bus trip for a dollar.

It felt like the phone rang a hundred times. Suddenly, a lady with a deep harsh voice answered.

"Hello! – Who is this?"

I could barely get my name to come out, "Deborah! May I please speak to my father?

"Who is your father?"

"Edward Jones," I softly replied,

"You don't have a daddy here and don't ever call my house again" click the phone went dead and so did my heart.

Many years have passed since my father was cut out of my life. He is now deceased. Now that I think about it, the time shared with him was all brief moments of pleasure. Was I naive? Did I fail to understand that a father was more than pleasure and one who gave gifts to their child? There were times we would ride the bus to my father's barber shop a few times a week for a dollar and we would rather walk from Overtown Miami, near the downtown area, on 20th Street to 65th Street just to save a dime from that same dollar. Just to keep that whole dollar felt like he was with us.

We craved small talk, as we enjoyed fast food from the local Royal Castle—hamburgers and root beer soda, what a meal. It felt good to have him as my father, especially since he allowed me to sit in his personal barber chair. I could turn in it anytime I wanted to and sitting in his chair was like sitting in his arms. There were times I went to the hairdresser and made my requests to her. Please don't shave my neck; my father wants to do that. It was a method to spend more time with him or just to sit in his chair.

Considering that my father was a well-known barber, his friends considered him to be "razor sharp." There were many reasons; he was always well groomed, handsome to look upon, and had a wealth of gold in his mouth. There were all sorts of designs on his teeth, stars, half moons, full crowns, and solid gold. Oh! —and when he smiled, his gold teeth captured your full attention. Gold teeth were a sign of wealth back in the days (now it's all about the hype). Both my brother and I crowned our teeth and to our surprise, we both longed to mirror his reflection. My brother was always well dressed and groomed. Moreover, I was attractive to tall well-dressed men, eventually marrying a well-dressed attractive man, but I always reminded him, *"I did not marry my father, so please don't act like him."* Many times women will marry the father whom they never had and it simply does not work- husbands are just that, our husbands and fathers or *baby daddies* to our children.

As I reflect deeper, my maternal father was never there emotionally for us. He never went to a school play, or took us to a park, or even a trip to Disneyland. As a matter of fact, our names never made his obituary and everyone knew we were his only children; still they failed to recognize us as his descendents, adding another cut to my heart. The children of married men did not get to enjoy full benefits of their maternal father, nor their inheritance. I guess that is how they did things back in the late fifty's and early sixty's. None of that matters to me, for I will always hold a place for him in my heart. When my brother speaks ill of him, my heart saddens. Not for my father, but for my brother who reminds me of him so often. Particularly, when my brother turns and walks away, the silhouette from his body radiates the image of my father and that's what gives the both of us the most pain. I feel my brother has never healed and has all but acknowledged the fact that mothers shared some of the responsibility. The fact is, our father was a married man, besides the subject never has come up between us regarding responsibility. It's time we move forward and accept some things we cannot change in order to live in freedom. I am reminded that it is the Truth that sets you free.

> *"All emotions are, to a greater or lesser degree, forceful, arousing, motivating, and hard to put under voluntary control. They always have a quality of pleasure (joy, love, pride) or the opposite (disgust, fury, dejection). Each emotion tends to be triggered by a characteristic set of stimuli—praise usually evokes happiness or pride, and loss evokes sadness—but the same stimulus will evoke a different emotional reaction depending upon an individual's temperament and circumstances. Praise can cause some people to feel ashamed or sad,* [3]

"And we know that all things work together for good to them that love God, to them who are the called according to his purpose."

Romans 8:28 KJV

GENERATION Z –SECRET WEAPON

Very few of us are prepared to deal with an emotionally challenged child, which makes it difficult to handle the harsh realities behind our own emotions. Typically, it's these frightening and frustrating issues that makes us react emotionally to today's generation.

The reason we become so emotionally reactive is that we take ourselves out of the present moment and the current issue we are facing.

Could this be happening again, fighting, cursing, yelling out, kicking and having to stop the car and watch him act out his unmet needs? Was it possible that I was too stubborn to give in? On the other hand, was it just simpler for me to call 911 for help as so many others do? How could this be happening to me? There were days when I felt more like a victim than a grandmother, as my own blood was becoming a public embarrassment.

Reflecting back on a Sunday afternoon when he accidently hit his head while diving in the pool. Of course it was his decision to dive in, when instructed not to and it was an accident; however, he blamed those around him for his painful experience. An experience that felt like World War III, especially after he witness both 'adults' and children laughing at him as he held his head. One would think that the adults would reach out and help him, check for swelling, blood or just do something. Instead, the adults joined in laughing at the site of child in pain. Pain that wasn't articulated -just filled with emotions and facial expressions and that's when all *hell* broke out.

In search of a mature masculine figure to help me calm him down emotionally. I hastily drove to my brother's house, hoping that he may be the one to help relieve the tension between us. I was praying that he would calmly speak to him regarding his behavior and possibly take on the task of mentoring him with words of wisdom. What I got was my brother yelling at this child and his advice to me was sounding like this, "You're going to catch a case-with this boy." I was like- what was I doing here, looking for hope and received disappointment. You don't calm down a person by yelling when they are emotional- let him melt down with understanding his pain. Where was the wisdom of the masculine male that I sought after?

Finally, a witness to what I was experiencing emotionally from a child, a child who learned to use profanity to describe his pain and emotions. Later that night I felt guilty that I was the enabler to his pain. It was my fault that I never explained to my family the emotional side of him. For fear they would use authority and control, the same as our parents and that's opposite to what an emotional child needs.

Amazingly, my brother reminded me of Deac, my stepfather, as I witnessed, little (if any) understanding of a troubled child.

EMOTIONAL CONNECTION OF THE DOLLAR

We both were being held captive to our emotions and unmet needs. He needed to fill a void and I was attached to my past. Eventually, I was able to listen to his behavior. I was amazed to discover the emotional connection or root behind his emotions and my anger; a *dollar bill*. I hated to hear him say, "Can I have a dollar?" Words like these were mental triggers to our emotional battles. I could predict the next scene, but emotionally, I could do nothing about the situation. I was charged from my own personal struggles and with it came cruel emotions.

As time passed, I eventually learned to initiate conversations with anyone and strangers were not exempt to the healing process. Besides, strangers seemed to offer the best counsel, empathy, and compassion to my hopeless situation. Was it because they all had similar situations and fear no longer bonded them to share their personal experiences?

I could not believe I was living with another strong-willed child; however, this time it was a child that was enmeshed with emotionally challenges. How could God be so unjust to me? I felt like Jonah when he cried out to God "O Lord, give ear to my prayer and take my life from me; for death is better for me than life." I desired *absolute* peace and at this point, peace could have been heavenly. I felt, my part of helping him was done, I did enough and my guilt was over. I had worked out my salvation and was ready for my reward. This was about the time my life was in need of a drastic change, a change that would include a *"realistic-moral inventory."* My attitude and beliefs about life, family and God were being challenged. I knew if change was ever going to occur in my family it had to start with me and with this came the truth of sorrow and suffering in my life. My change came slowly so I could share my experiences with others without shame, as darkness no longer covered me with despair and fear. Light was now coming and shining in, like daybreak.

> *Many times when we look at the word moral, we think of it as having something to do with sex, stealing, or lying. It is much more that. Our prejudices, intolerance, criticisms, fears, and guilt are all part of our morality, as are selfishness, egotism, and resentment. Morality should come from within us. It comes from beliefs and attitudes which we have accepted as truths, from childhood. In growing up, we may have acquired guilt, shame, or embarrassment for our thoughts, feelings, and experiences, and we need to bring these tormenting ghosts out into the open.[4]*

It wasn't hard for me to imagine what he was feeling. It's been more that twenty nine- years since I woke up at my aunt house. I don't remember driving there, although what I do remember is feeling the presence of a stronger force standing over me. The authority projecting from their presence was so cold to me. I laid there with my eyes closed as family members discussed me as if I was an object. I could hear announced interrogations, rushing over my head, as my aunt attempted to explain many reasons she felt for my coming to her house. If they only knew how I was feeling, already ashamed for my behavior. I had to add the verdict of being judged and condemned.

As she was explaining to them, one of my aunt's neighbors knocked on the door, for she witnessed my car scraping one of the street poles. I felt my aunt's neighbor had more concern for me than my own family. How could that be? For some, it may feel like the neighbor was late in her arriving, but for me, she was on time to focus them on a larger issue, me.

Suddenly, I was awoken by the handshakes of an older sibling, "What is your problem?" A tone that I heard before, harsh and cold, and then I could feel I was an embarrassment to the family, again. It's interesting, but I realized that most of my family has a temperament of conflict, particularly if we wore on the family through public embarrassment.

WOMEN SUFFER TOO

After attending several Emotions Anonymous (EA) meetings, I had the pleasure to met people from all walks of life. People who were willing to be real with themselves by admitting they encountered emotional challenges and fears. EA meetings were a safe place to share emotional issues openly without fear of being rejected or someone telling you to "Just trust in the Lord everything will be alright". When they knew deep within themselves, they preferred not to hear emotional issues because of their own. My emotional pain was real and I needed to know that there were others in this world, which was experiencing some of the same issues that plagued me. My life was no longer classroom theory it was life and trusting God seemed difficult some of the time, particularly in my own home.

Exhausted by the thought of defeat, one day while sitting at my desk, lost in solitude, I resigned to glance upward and in the midst of clutter was a little blue book. A colleague had given it to me for its insightful techniques. He had hoped it would aid me in reaching out to others, particularly, those who were unable to manage their personal conflicts in the workplace. Today, I realize he was reaching out to me, as I was the one in need of help. My suffering was causing problems and emotional plights that were noticeable by someone who truly cared for my mental health and family.

Many times we sit in the midst of people for years and never connect to their suffering. Mostly likely, because one would have to get in the midst of a painful experience, in efforts to understand what they are dealing with. Unresolved hurts and unmet needs may take on the form of a disease or addiction and many of us are plagued with them both. As I began to look within the pages of this little blue book, I found these words, which describes my feelings and frustrations, as it was time to deal with these tormenting ghosts:

> *I was bitterly unhappy…I was convinced that I was having a serious mental breakdown. I wanted help…. I began to get a picture of myself, of the temperament that had caused me so much trouble. I had been hypersensitive, shy, and idealistic. My inability to accept the harsh realities of life had resulted in a disillusioned cynic, clothed in a protective armor against the world's misunderstandings. That armor had turned into prison walls, locking me in loneliness—and fear. All I had left*

was an iron determination to live my own life in spite of the alien world—and here I was, an inwardly frightened, outwardly defiant woman, who desperately needed a prop to keep going….

I wasn't the only person in the world who felt and behaved like this! I wasn't mad or vicious…… I was an intellectual and I needed an intellectual answer, not an emotional one…. and the light streamed in. I wasn't trapped. I wasn't helpless, I was free… free from anger and fear, freedom to know happiness and love.

There is another meaning for the Hebrew word that in the King James Version of the Bible is translated "salvation." It is "to come home." I had found my salvation. I wasn't alone anymore. That was the beginning of a new life, fuller life, a happier life than I had ever known, or believed possible. I had found friends, understanding friends who often knew what I was thinking and feeling better than I knew myself, and didn't allow me to retreat into my prison of loneliness and fear over a fancied slight or hurt… Talking things over with them, great floods of enlightenment showed me myself as I really was and I was like them. We all had hundreds of character traits, of fears and phobias, likes and dislikes in common. Suddenly I could accept myself, faults and all, as I was— for weren't we all like that? Moreover, accepting this, I felt a new inner comfort, and the willingness and strength to do something about the traits I couldn't live with… The felling of impending disaster that had haunted me for years began to dissolve as I put into practice more and more of the Twelve Steps… I have something to contribute to humanity, since I am peculiarly qualified, as a fellow-suffer, to give aid and comfort to those who have stumbled and fallen … over this business of….life …. [5]

One day, out of nowhere I started to share intimate memories regarding my childhood and present day issues. What a relief to be in an organized setting sharing my innermost feelings. EA became my family and I soon realized that people of all ethnic backgrounds have similar feelings toward family, friends, self, and God, but something was different about this group of people, they had a desire to become well emotionally.

An Emotions Anonymous program has been known to work miracles in the lives of many who suffer from problems as diverse as depression, anger, broken or strained relationships, grief, anxiety, low self-esteem, panic, abnormal fears, resentment, jealousy, guilt, despair, fatigue, tension, boredom, loneliness, withdrawal, obsessive and negative thinking, worry, compulsive behavior, and a variety of other emotional issues.[6]

After many visits with my emotions, I realized that letting go of emotional suffering is a choice. Although at times, it didn't feel that simple. Our lives are very complex and some of us have to unlearn behaviors and learn how to make new choices if we want relief from past experiences. The world is filled with all kinds of people; people who are just like you and I, searching for that special someone endowed with godly wisdom and having the ability to empathically listen as we express our emotional pain.

I diligently searched until I found godly wisdom, so I could care for a child who relied on me and my family to lead him to the Master Healer, The Christ. He needed someone in the flesh who would ease his pain, by not adding any more pain to his young life. This child was a tender branch from a dry tree, which appeared like an olive tree, strong, wise, silently hearing many secrets that allowed him to withstand the storms of life. Besides, who gave me the right to be angry with God? Blame my family for not understanding my fears and to feel sorry for myself!

Before long, I found enough strength to encourage myself, stop my complaints to a sovereign God and express my gratitude for sending a child to teach me that I had unfinished emotional issues. I made a commitment to think of the good in my life and release the negatives and sufferings to a loving Savior. It was time for me to relearn how to be grateful to a Sovereign God and thank Him for putting supportive people in my life, during such a difficult time. I repented for the spirit of error, resigned my will to God's perfect will, my mind to the mind of Christ and my emotions to the person and the stable working of the Holy Spirit.

Being powerless felt good for the first time, as I knew that my Savior was carrying me. It was refreshing for me to give my burdens to the Lord and that included my entire family's unstable emotions. I was not God, nor his Son, as I could not battle my emotions in my own strength. My emotional battle had others tied to its past. It was time for me to learn the true nature of God as the Father, Jesus as his Son and Holy Spirit's power to heal and restore health.

Chapter 7

A Closer Look

And they came to Beth-saida. And they took a blind man to him, requesting him to put his hands on him. And he took the blind man by the hand, and went with him out of the town; and when he had put water from his mouth on his eyes, and put his hands on him, he said, Do you see anything? Then again he put his hands on his eyes; and looking hard, he was able to see, and saw all things clearly. And he sent him away to his house, saying, Do not even go into the town.

Mark 8:22-26 BEE

A CLOSER LOOK

I could no longer make unreasonable demands on others when I was the one in need of a reality check. For the first time I was truly looking in the mirror and not liking what was being reflected. It was time for a change, as there was no longer a reason to be ridged, controlling and demanding. I discovered that the spirit of 'manipulation' had an entire family in bondage and it was time to get it from lurking in hidden places within my heart.

Leo Buscaglia describes in his book *Love;* Love is like a mirror, when you love another you become his mirror and he becomes yours. Real love always creates, it never destroys.

"In fact, the fear of aloneness and lack of love is so great in most of us that it's possible we can become a slave of this fear. If so, we're ready to part with even our true self, anything, to meet others' needs and in this way hope to gain intimate companionship for ourselves. We need others. We need others to love and we need to be loved by them. There is no doubt that without it, we too, like the infant left alone, would cease to grow, cease to develop, choose madness and even death"[1]

SHATTERING STRONGHOLDS

Emotions have a significant impact on the body with feelings from the top of the head to the sole of the feet. For some of us, emotions can cause physical illness where physicians cannot determine the true cause behind its manifestation. Emotions could have a connection to perfume, a familiar face or even a place. A painful memory could trigger an emotional reaction anywhere and anytime. Emotions also have spiritual connections and can hinder your relationship with a Loving God.

There was a time in my life when I struggled academically, socially, and emotionally. There were days my emotions manifested into physical pain. It was these same emotions that overwhelmed me during the holidays, especially when I was emotionally *forced* to attend family functions. I would be so fearful of family jokes, that my body would do amazing things; I would physically get sick, blood pressure rising for no apparent reason, feet and ankles would swell including digestive problems and headaches. There were times my memory would even have short lapses. I would forget where my keys to the car and house were, when they were gently placed in my purse. My husband would remind me to keep my *things in one place* and for me my purse was that safe place. Nonetheless, when I looked there the keys would disappear. My poor husband had no idea as to what was happening to me. The internal stress of the thought of family jokes caused me to physically breakdown prior to family functions.

One day I had a crash course on discernment and the Holy Spirit was my teacher. My relationships and reactions were related to my childhood experiences with my father and these experiences were the fuel for hurt and anger to raise its repulsive head. My behavior was erratic, irresponsible and I was having tantrums, if things did not go exactly my way. My poor husband loved me the more, as he managed to shake his head in grief, hoping everyone would just leave me alone. He was willing to stay home with me alone just so I would not physically and emotionally get out of control.

At one point, I became stressed out because I was not prospering financially. I truly believed God had abandoned me. I was giving to the church, people and those in need. There were brief drops of blessings but nothing actually manifested to relieve my financial burdens, my finances merely got worst. Can I keep it real for a minute! Malachi 3:10 was no longer *my* verse of choice. *"Bring ye all the tithes into the storehouse, that there may be meat in mine house, and prove me now herewith, saith the LORD of hosts, if I will not open you the windows of heaven, and pour you out a blessing, that there shall not be room enough to receive it"* (KJV).

> *"The Lord hates people who use dishonest scales. He is happy with honest weights."*
>
> ### Proverbs 11:1 GNT

The difference between my grandson and I varied between how anger was being express openly. His anger would lead him to an emotional rage which lasted about twenty minutes and it was over, as if nothing ever happened. On the other hand, I was physically, emotionally and spiritually harboring anger with thoughtful resentment. After all, I was doing. Even questioning God, "Why was I being held captive for something out of my control? An answer came back clear and strong. "I was doing the providing in my own strength, and this type of anger had spiritual connections."

I vowed to God, to *study –not read* the book of Proverbs for 100 days and to give my spiritual leader a dollar a day until the stronghold of a dollar bill was shattered physically and spiritually. I was desperate and needed the assurance that God would hear my prayers. *"And she vowed a vow, and said, O LORD of hosts, if thou wilt indeed look on the affliction of thine handmaid, and remember me, and not forget thine handmaid… Praise waiteth for thee, O God, in Sion: and unto thee shall the vow be performed (Samuel 1:11: Psalm 65:1 KJV)*

Later that evening, I listened as a child shared his personal feelings with me. Caught off guard, that he was willing to share his insight, not realizing which way this could go, I mention a few boundaries. According to his personal assessment of our relationship, "You know what, you don't understand children, and you're not mature and need to calm down! You need to be more compassionate with me and think about my life." I was furious as if Satan himself stood up in me, replying emotionally, "I'm a grown woman- what do you mean – I'm not mature- I am taking care of you, aren't I!" Then with a humbled heart, I knew he was right. A child was telling me how he felt and this time I had to listen to him- out of the mouth of babes truth and honesty.

Sometimes it's better to understand, than be understood.

He was telling me the truth about me. It was like looking through a glass mirror and the reflection was not pleasant to the eyes. I was angry with God for not delivering on His promise regarding material blessings. Was I unable to fulfill the requests of a child or was he asking too much of me?

I never knew what a compassionate person looked or felt like. I only saw one from a distance. I felt like my mother shared her love towards her children with varied affections, so how could I understand? I could only remember embracing her on visits after I was a grown woman! It was clear that neither of us ever experienced unconditional love and affection. Could it be that I learned if you work hard and demand respect that was love? God's words are true; *a good person is no better off than a sinner.* It was time to push past symbolic love and embrace unconditional love.

MY OWN STUFF

"Gold and silver are tested by fire, and a person's heart is tested by the Lord." I found myself doubting God and His Son, Jesus' ability to rescue me from my pain. Desiring more of God and His treasures came with a price. To make Him the center of my life would require an intentional effort on my part. To know Him personally would require me to keep my focus on the Redeemer and His cross. In his book, *Seeing and Savoring Jesus Christ,* John Piper says:

> *If we exchange God's glory for lesser things, he gives us up to lived-out parables of depravity-the other exchanges that mirror, in our misery, the ultimate sellout... We were made to know and treasure the glory of God above all things; and when we trade that treasure for images, everything is disordered. The sun of God's glory was made to shine at the center of the solar system of our soul. And when it does, all the planets of our life are held in their proper orbit. But when the sun is displaced,*

everything flies apart. The healing of the soul begins by
restoring the glory of God to its flaming, all-attracting
place at the center.[2]

I was tired of working in my own strength and relapsing emotionally. My heart and mind was not working as one with God. I was so determined to prove to others, my strength in a spiritual war; a war that wasn't meant for me to fight alone. I soon realized that Jesus was the only one who could defeat Satan and his demons who fought for our souls. When the battle cry sounded, my feet had to wear Jesus' sandals of peace and my garments must include the Word of Truth, faith and praise.

THE CONFLICT OF TEMPERAMENTS

I was living in the flesh and praying in the spirit. What has come over me! My will was not presenting itself in a delightful or honorable manner. Hostile emotions surrounded our home and it consumed all involved in the battle. It felt like a military take-over and we were losing ground to the enemy. Why were we thinking evil in our hearts, when it's easier to say, "I love you and would never give up on you". Could we honestly judge and condemn when our own hearts and thoughts were in conflict within our bodies? Could it be that Jesus would be honored in our lives so that others may know that the Son of Man has authority on earth to forgive sins, regardless of our spiritual, physical and emotional condition? There were some things that could not be altered; we were fearfully and wonderfully created by God. Unique from the womb in the care of the Creator and there will always be mysteries. Some things we do not understand in the spiritual and physical nature of man.

We know that the Law is spiritual; but I am a mortal,
sold as a slave to sin. I do not understand what I do; for

I don't do what I would like to do, but instead I do what I hate. Since what I do is what I don't want to do, this shows that I agree that the Law is right. So I am not really the one who does this thing; rather it is the sin that lives in me. I know that good does not live in me—that is, in my human nature. For even though the desire to do good is in me, I am not able to do it. I don't do the good I want to do; instead, I do the evil that I do not want to do. If I do what I don't want to do, this means that I am no longer the one who does it; instead, it is the sin that lives in me.

So I find that this law is at work: when I want to do what is good, what is evil is the only choice I have. My inner being delights in the law of God. But I see a different law at work in my body—a law that fights against the law which my mind approves of. It makes me a prisoner to the law of sin which is at work in my body. What an unhappy man I am! Who will rescue me from this body that is taking me to death? Thanks be to God, who does this through our Lord Jesus Christ! This, then, is my condition: on my own I can serve God's law only with my mind, while my human nature serves the law of sin. (Romans 7: 14-25 GNT)

My life was beginning to be a little clearer, that is to say, my flesh was giving me the problem. There were weakness within my temperament that tended to focus on mistakes and the negatives of others, including myself. Needless to say, we live in the flesh. We breathe air, need relationships, require shelter, eat and need love. Humans are not divine! Nevertheless, there was a spiritual side that longed to be connected to a loving Father. Desperately desiring to do God's will, needless to say my emotions were at war with my divine assignment. It was several months before a 'Christian Counselor' suggested temperament.

Whatever the conflict that was keeping us disconnected had to be dealt with quickly. All of us were hoping that things would settle down, so that we could provide him with a stable home environment and a fresh outlook at life.

I prayed that our temperaments were similar, so we all could begin to thrive in an atmosphere of peace and joy – as soon as he realized that we loved him. Anything, as long as it would reduce conflict between us and in our home. I knew the temperament analysis would eliminate unnecessary strife and improve our quality of life if nothing else, but there was always a possibility that our temperaments could clash- and they did! He was out going, socially oriented and verbally expressive and I was an introvert and a loner. He did not want to be controlled and I thrived in controlling.

If our assignment was to aid in his care, then we needed to understand each other's natural tendencies and how to best satisfy those unmet needs, in order to eliminate stress and tension within our home. In order to manage some emotional conflicts, Temperament Analysis Profiles were used as one of the ways to pinpoint the true source of our troubles. Unfortunately, there were severe gaps between his temperament and his actual behavior. His anxiety levels had influenced his behavior, along with the force of risk factors that only manifested more problems.

> *And we have given up the secret things of shame, not walking in false ways, and not making use of the word of God with deceit; but by the revelation of what is true, as before God, we have the approval of every man's sense of right and wrong. But if our good news is veiled, it is veiled from those who are on the way to destruction: Because the god of this world has made blind the minds of those who have not faith, so that the light of the good news of*

the glory of Christ, who is the image of God, might not be shining on them. For our preaching is not about ourselves, but about Christ Jesus as Lord, and ourselves as your servants through Jesus. Seeing that it is God who said, Let light be shining out of the dark, who has put in our hearts the light of the knowledge of the glory of God in the face of Jesus Christ. But we have this wealth in vessels of earth, so that it may be seen that the power comes not from us but from God; Troubles are round us on every side, but we are not shut in; things are hard for us, but we see a way out of them; We are cruelly attacked, but not without hope; we are made low, but we are not without help.

(*2 Corinthians 4:2-9BBE*)

BELIEVE IN THE INVISIBLE

I listened to a gentle voice challenge me declaring, "My seed is blessed and change was possible." "Look past what you see",- "look beyond pain, hurt and fear." Was this all an illusion? Was I blind to God's glory and what was happening in my family? The Lord Himself was answering my prayers and I had to put my hope in Him. If we are to find peace with our past, some of us may have to revisit it in order to shut the door on a past that keeps interfering with relationships with others. God has people who are filled with godly wisdom, people who are better able to assist you in understanding the conflict that lives in the midst of despair and hope.

When I think of all the frustrating moments in my life, the best breakthroughs were when I helped others in their search for hope. However, it was not until this particular day I was introduced to the healing light of God, a marvelous light that shinned down from heaven into my dark and wounded heart. This must have been how the Apostle Paul came alive when he was in those dark prison cells, writing and encouraging others to hold fast to the blessed Hope. It was this light of hope that kept the Apostle connected to the mind of Christ.

The method that God uses to get our attention is not always comfortable. This fundamental principle is the one that gives us the most pain. If we are to break the cycle of pain within our family, then we must get to the root cause of our problems. God will not allow brokenness to feed brokenness. It's not easy. Regardless of the situation we're in, we can learn the secret of being "content" and that is, being in union with God.

> *In my life in union with the Lord it is a great joy to me that after so long a time you once more had the chance of showing that you care for me. I don't mean that you had stopped caring for me—you just had no chance to show it. And I am not saying this because I feel neglected, for I have learned to be satisfied with what I have. I know what it is to be in need and what it is to have more than enough. I have learned this secret, so that anywhere, at any time, I am content, whether I am full or hungry, whether I have too much or too little. I have the strength to face all conditions by the power that Christ gives me.*

(Philippians 4:10-13 GNT)

HELPING THE ONE WHO NEED IT THE MOST

I was at a crossroads ready to throw in the towel and feeling discouraged because I had not seen any results of our labor. Our life was turned upside down. I was beginning to wear down from medical appointments. This particular week was extremely difficult for both of us, as emotional behaviors took on the appearance of defiance and control. Besides, this child's heart was not with us anymore.

He was yearning to reunite with his mother and today my feelings were mutual. We spend so much time taking young children out of homes, instead of training young parents to care for their home. There is something seriously wrong with this picture, best practices and the study of behavior.

One day an elderly lady said to me "you will understand it better by and by." These words help me to understand the challenges of life's demands and God's timing. It's not up to me to determine when the Lord will answer my prayers; it's about life's lessons on the way to prayers being answered.

God has the leading role in our lives and some things just take a little longer because of life's demands. No matter what we are to put our trust in the Savior, even the things we don't understand.

Chapter 8
Can't Make it Without the Lord

Let it be all joy to you, my brothers, when you undergo tests of every sort; Because you have the knowledge that the testing of your faith gives you the power of going on in hope; But let this power have its full effect, so that you may be made complete, needing nothing. But if any man among you is without wisdom, let him make his request to God, who gives freely to all without an unkind word, and it will be given to him. Let him make his request in faith, doubting nothing; for he who has doubt in his heart is like the waves of the sea, which are troubled by the driving of the wind. Let it not seem to such a man that he will get anything from the Lord; For there is a division in his mind, and he is uncertain in all his ways. But let the brother of low position be glad that he is lifted up; There is a blessing on the man who undergoes testing; because, if he has God's approval, he will be given the crown of life, which the Lord has said he will give to those who have love for him.

James 1: 2-12 BBE

CAN'T MAKE IT WITHOUT THE LORD

Returning to work after a long discussion regarding my frustrations at home and the vicarious situation, I was in with my

Administrator. His soft words of wisdom were like a message from God Himself, just *"change the towel."* It was time to stir up my faith and rid my mind of doubt and unbelief. I had to get a firm grip on God's unconditional love. If the family was going to accept this enormous change in our home, changing had to start with me. I could no longer look weary or wear a frown on my face. In the midst of what my natural eyes were seeing, I had to set the tone for my family.

*"Change within do not come over night,
however, if you keep at it the heart, mind, and
soul should eventually be stirred."*

Dr. Martin L. King

INDIVIDUAL RESPONSIBILITY

The times we live in are different. Within our family, each one of us has a responsibility to future generations. There is a generation blaming their absent fathers and cursing their mothers. A generation whose motives are not pure in the eyesight of God who thinks they're better than others are by putting people down and judging them.

Is it the parent's fault our children live in fear and shame, receiving the short end of life because they are without fathers in the home? We teach our children to, "Honor thy mother and father so your days may be long in the earth", but who is the child's father and better yet where is the mother to fulfill this promise?

There is a possibility that we are living in denial as to what's happening around us, until we hear about the one that is being sexually abused, placed in foster care, taken to juvenile or youth selling drugs on our streets! Could someone teach them to love the Lord and to fear Him or is it all about honoring parents who are not in the home? Everywhere you turn; there are whispers from adults with complaints regarding future generations. However, it is always coming from those who are not willing to take responsibility for all their mistakes. The irony is all of us are helping our children learn how to manage their emotions.

A young man stepped (meaning-walked up) to me one day and shared with me his life story. A story he apparently longed to share for some time. He wanted to tell someone the truth behind his pain, anger and leaving school before graduating, but he was too afraid to do so. He feared someone would judge his mother. Struggling to ask for help, he admitted to me that he did not know *how* to ask for help, partly because he never had to ask. He was forced to accept life as it was. He wanted out of his current lifestyle. He had enough of people judging him for not completing his education, failing to attend church and blaming him for the declining moral ethics within our society.

I listened in silence as pain echoed from within him; he sounded off on me that day as he opened up his broken heart. According to him, it was impossible for me or anyone to understand anything about his life; a life rooted in pain.

"You think people care about me! Do people know I can hear them talking about me? They judge me by what they see-people don't know my heart; they just look at me and judge, and these are the same people you're talking to me about, *'church people!'* These people talk about us in the store, in the church, at school, at work, on the bus, and at the flea market. They don't care about us! They care about themselves! I hear their comments, thinking they are better than we are and why do people go to church anyway. They sure aren't praying for me! You see I hurt too."

From my point of view, this young man was smart, gifted in technology and very articulate. He stood tall and had the courage to challenge my beliefs about a generation. A generation who hungered for a better life and if given the opportunity, they were willing to turn their backs on a lifestyle they came to know. That day, I learned a very important life lesson, which is, *"Let no one despise your youth."*

Our youth of today are gifted, talented, and waiting for an opportunity to display their gifts and talents. Unfortunately, they have many roadblocks that prevent them from doing so. In the midst of unresolved emotional pain, some of them have aged out of foster care and left to themselves or to find their own way.

Pain has a purpose and that is to teach each of us how to endure the tests of life. The more difficult the pain, the more time it takes to heal and to uncover the layers of unresolved hurts. Regardless if you are able to handle power, wealth, and success, many adults have unresolved childhood hurts that they are passing on to another generation. In order for adults to meet the challenges of today's generation, we will have to walk in unconditional love and make a heart decision to do so and that's only if we desire our children's children to take part in the final wedding banquet.

There is a generation engulfed in pain and sorrow and many of them are without the nurturance of a mother and father in their home. They lack guidance and someone to have patience with them. The Lord challenged me after this young man helped me to understand his willingness to change. He had energy that surrounded him and was confident that somehow with or without my help he will survive. I almost missed an opportunity to influence a generation and bear much fruit as commanded of me. God knew the ending of this young man's life before the story was written. He knows our ending and has made provision for us as well.

> *"When my father and my mother are turned away from me, then the Lord will be my support."*

FAMILIAR SPIRITS

Early one Sunday morning, a familiar knock was requesting entrance into my heart and mind. I made a decision not to let any more tormenting demons come to cloud my judgment in order to confuse me and lead me astray. I was stronger now and made a decision to trust God. I was ready to move forward and embrace my emotional freedom. I was tired of living in a dark past, a past that only wanted to remind me of a broken heart. It was time to put an end to these tormenting demons of fear and shame. I could feel that they were in for an unusual encounter with the Holy One of Israel. They were about to meet the healing power of Jesus in my life. I was going to go forward and retrieve my future. A future God had ordained for me before time.

I refused to live a life resigned to torment; a life with the possibilities of ruining my family's relationship. Having few personal relationships and not accepting help from others because of the gripping fear that shame had on me. I feared someone would find out the truth about my past and I was now ashamed of this child's inward pain. I desperately wanted to help my family and others understand their emotions in a godly way. Then a spirit of hope and a promise from God, spoke gently to my heart, "You're a good candidate to help others, for you have decided that Scriptures are true and they can be trusted".

*All things work together for good to them that
love God.*

Romans 8:28, KJV

The power of God had not come upon me to do the work that was involved to care for His people. I had to wait to be sent forth, as His Word became alive and active to my whole body and soul. If I was going to proclaim Truth and be effective it would take the power of God. As hearts were hardened by the cares of this world, it would take a compassionate person clothe in unconditional love to reach people who were contaminated with tormenting spirits and bleeding hearts. I had to battle with my eyes fixed on Jesus. Not the kind you might be thinking of, like turning water into wine as I did during my naive days, but God's power to access an unconditional and anointing love, whose healing leaves was able to heal nations. Yes, I too had to wait before I could share my story.

Now that I think about it, even the disciples encountered fear and shame. These men of God ate dinner and witnessed His miracles and sometimes felt they were unworthy to proclaim the Good News. There are many more ordinary people like you and me, whose life has been marred and oppressed by fear and shame.

DELIVERANCE FROM THE TWINS

I was tormented by my past. I was behind prison walls held captive by the twins fear and shame. Anger was their correctional officers and guilt was the warden. Despair, rejection, pride and doubt made regular visits to my mind many times, on a daily basis because I allow them too. I refused to forgive the people who hurt me. Fear and shame were like a cancer going undetected for years.

It was hard for me to make changes when I was full of fear. Could it be that I doubted God's ability to deliver me from the hands of the oppressor, or just doubted that He cares for someone like me. I was tired of going to church and returning home with a quarter of a tank of gas with just enough of the message on Sunday to get me through Wednesday about noon. I desired to be free from all this. People around me could not help because they were having the same problems, but there was a difference I was transparent and I had enough of being driven by fear.

In his book, The Impossible Just Takes A Little Longer: Living with Purpose and Passion, *Art Berg writes, "In fact, fear is the main factor that stops so many of you from capitalizing on opportunities. It is what keeps you from making any significant improvement in your life. It is what makes you live your life through the expectations of others rather than listen to your heart and pursue a vision of yourself for which you have real passion. It is fear that has made you decide that it is still best to live reactively from day to day, sheltering yourselves, staying paralyzed. As a result, you spend more time trying to avoid life's challenges than facing them. You know that transforming your life can produce anxiety, and because anxiety frightens you, you back off altogether. Even if you find yourself thrown by life into horrible circumstances, it's still scary to begin the process of changing to get out of those circumstances."[1]*

Salvation is a freedom that even Prophets searched for diligently. It's time for a generation of believers to embrace His healing power and allow Him to strip us from the weights of this world and a tormenting past. This could be possible, when He lives in our hearts. The same healing power that flowed through Jesus to open blind eyes and deaf ears are available today.

All of us were given a measure of faith and it will take this pure faith, which is more precious than gold, to help us. The truth is that we must not get discouraged in our prayer time to the Father. When things get difficult in our lives, He doesn't want us to change our prayers. He wants us to remain faithful to the Scriptures when we pray and believe. It is only by God's grace and His Son's blood that we can forgive others and get our deliverance.

Chapter 9

Misguided Pain

> *"Homes are made by the wisdom of women,*
> *but are destroyed by foolishness."*
>
> ### Proverbs 14:1GNT

MISGUIDED PAIN

As God began to reveal His truths unto me, everywhere I turned the signs were there. My husband had in his power to bless his family and block the attacks of the enemy from seeping into our home. However, I failed him by preventing or blocking him from taking his rightful position as priest of our home. It was all because of a painful past and unresolved hurts from my childhood. I was extremely aggressive requiring my husband to do things on *my* timetable. Oh yes, I love my husband; there is no doubt to my love *(It's just, he never appeared to move fast enough for me)*.

I was a professional nag, complaining either that he was not studying the Bible long enough, letting things breakdown, and not repairing them or not helping me discipline the children, again all on my timetable. There was always something to do, particularly when he was watching too much television. My *'honey do list'* went on and on and on. I was the typical frustrated woman with unresolved issues and unmet needs.

My emotions were about to destroy my home and cause me to walk out, leaving my husband and my home. 'Leave my husband and a father to my children'! What was I thinking of? I truly loved and respected him for loving me unconditionally all these years.

My behavior was inconsistent with the Word of God and to make things worse I would sing that old familiar song, "What's love got to do with it?" I was a *hot mess*! Allowing guilt and shame to divide my home, I changed towels all right, just to pick one with an accusatory spirit attached to it. There was always something negative for me to say, blind to the good he did. My behavior went on like this for years. Now that I look back, had my husband not ignored my behavior, I was a good candidate to play 'How do you have a destructive relationship and enter the domestic violence cycle?' I was a **strong** woman, unwilling to totally surrender or submit to my husband's leadership. An emotional war was raging within me. I was so angry that it was difficult to believe the problem existed within me.

My pain was going in the wrong direction and my dear husband was not the true problem- he was my support system. It never dawned on me, that my husband needed time for himself. My anger had a way of shutting down all my emotions. What would it cost me to be submissive? The truth is that it doesn't cost me anything. Unconditional love has no strings attached to it. Jesus made that clear on the cross. This was a humbling experience for me to surrender to my husband wholeheartedly. I no longer desired control in this area of my life. I needed the Lord's help to understand him. In other words, I did not have to see my husband perform to my standards; I had to believe in him as my husband.

Change is change; you just have to look for it. A wise lady gave me a golden nugget; any change is change. Then it happened! I had awakened just before dawn and noticed my husband on his knees praying. Then, one morning, I noticed him reading the Bible in silence. What was playing out vividly was spiritual, I was missing out on our early morning Bible studies together. We fail to adjust this link when our family embraced a new member. My ears were now open to hear him come home and thank God for another safe trip. He even praised God for his family and home. Suddenly, I realized how blessed I was to have a husband like him; one who loves God, his family and me!

Now more than ever my spirit was determined to discover what was holding me captive emotionally. There was something more that was lingering deep within my past and I had to *do the work* to find out the truth behind my anger and unstable emotions. I had to be willing to let it all go. Secrets of the past were haunting me, causing guilt, and condemnation. I had to come to terms with the fact that it was my unresolved issues that were dividing my home. The place I call my sanctuary.

The veil was immediately removed from my eyes, as I was doing the same disgusting things I accused others of—that was being a foolish wife! I had a contaminated heart and toxins were radiating guilt that was causing all my problems. Within my heart, I allowed a loving Savior to live in impoverished conditions. My heart was beautiful from a spectator point of view, happy, in control and sociable, but hidden was bitterness and deceit.

My home was being destroyed by the foolish things of this world, financial distress, high credit card debt, and longing for a deeper spiritual life. As a result, I was about to lose my family and home. The consequences of my behavior were negatively affecting my children and grandchildren. In the midst of it all I was being stripped of everything that I put more trust in, including material possessions. Besides that, my education was costing a small fortune. Even my career took a turn in the wrong direction and without warning; my blood pressure silently went up as I made frequent visits to the ER.

Rejecting the very same ones that came to me for help, my negative circumstances were being blame on everyone but me, refusing to acknowledge my part in what was entrusted to me. Nor was I willing to accept full responsibility for not waiting on God. I was caught up in the making things happen syndrome. Better yet, I had a "fake it till I make it mind set." Nothing appeared to be working in my favor, regardless of how much tithes and offerings were taken to the storehouse.

My spiritual sight was returning and my mind was open for renewal. Therefore, I started looking at others around me and what I found was both alarming and distressing. People 'attending' church were no better off than the wicked, poor and diseased. Church people had the same problems as the world. With one exception, *church* people were too ashamed to *ask for help!* Some were even falling away from the faith. What was wrong with this logic and reasoning? Either I trust God or I turn away from Him. It was time for me to make a decision.

As for me and my house, we will serve the LORD.

Joshua 24:15 KJV

"O God, I am too ashamed to raise my head in your presence. Our sins pile up higher than our heads; they reach as high as the heavens. From the days of our ancestors until now, us, your people have sinned greatly. Because of our sins our kings, our priests, and we have fallen into the hands of foreign kings, and we have been slaughtered, robbed, and carried away as prisoners. We have been totally disgraced, as we still are today. Now for a short time, O LORD our God, you have been gracious to us and have let some of us escape from slavery and live in safety in this holy place. You have let us escape from slavery and have given us new life. We were slaves, but you did not leave us in slavery. You made the emperors of Persia favor us and permit us to go on living and to rebuild your Temple, which was in ruins, and to find safety here in Judah and Jerusalem. But now, O God, what can we say after all that has happened? We have again disobeyed the commands that you gave us through your servants, the prophets. They told us that the land we were going to occupy was an impure land because the people who lived in it filled it from one end to the other with disgusting, filthy actions. They told us that we were never to intermarry with those people and never to help them prosper or succeed if we wanted to enjoy the land and pass it on to our descendants forever. Even after everything that has happened to us in punishment for our sins and wrong doings, we know that You, our God, have punished us less than we deserve and have allowed us to survive. Then how can we ignore your commandments again and intermarry with these wicked people? If we do, you will be so angry that you will destroy us completely and let no one survive.

LORD God of Israel, you are just, but you have let us survive. We confess our guilt to you; we have no right to come into your presence." (Ezra 9: 6- 15 GNT)

EXPOSED NOT EXPELLED

I found myself weeping and repenting for my sins, secrets, broken faith with God, and the sins of my ancestors. God made me a promise never to leave me or forsake me. That means my seed is blessed. I could have His blessings for a thousand generations, if I walk upright and have faith in God to redeem, heal and restore my family's faith. There was one condition that I let go and that included any spirits that controlled my emotions from the grave. It was my responsibility to become a doer of the Word of God, as the Spirit of Truth exposed my life.

> *"Darkness cannot drive out darkness; only light can do that. Hate cannot drive out hate; only love can do that."*

-Martin Luther King, Jr.

Was it possible to carry hurt from my childhood for all these years? My worst fear was my fear. My childhood was interfering with my ability to love and make peace with God. In meditation and a *simple honest prayer from the heart,* I made my confessions to God. I sat in silence waiting for the Holy Spirit to replace darkness with light, hate with love, and lies with truth. I felt a sharp pain in my chest. It felt like needles were being removed from my heart. As pressure was being released, a rush of serenity filled my heart. I fell to my knees, as tears streamed down my face, the Holy Spirit gently spoke to me, *"It's not your fault."* In the midst of my tears, God's TRUTH was revealed to me and there was sheer relief and the Father's reassurance of love. "Flesh and blood could not reveal this unto me, it can only be revealed by the Holy Spirit."

My inability to love was hindered by false truths. God is in me and has been all the time, for He has never left me nor forsaken me. The power of God overwhelmed my heart, mind and soul as His peace loved on my heart filling holes and dark spaces with the sweet aroma of a loving Savior's cross. All my issues were left at the cross. As I declared God's grace, grace and more grace. Now I understand that it was never the Lord's intention for any of us to carry heavy burdens alone. The day finally came for me to stop controlling my own pain. His Son has done this for me on the cross. His perfect love had finally come to heal my broken heart.

> *"Therefore judge nothing before the time, until the Lord come, who both will bring to light the hidden things of darkness, and will make manifest the counsels of the hearts: and then shall every man have praise of God. Light shineth in darkness; and the darkness comprehended it not."*

1 Corinthians, 4:5, KJV

The pains of the past for many are real. They haunt us by tormenting our emotions and ruining our relationships with God and others. The impact that unresolved pain has on one's life cannot be denied as they vary from person to person, including one's temperament, learned behaviors, personality and environment. The Apostle Paul reminds all of us to *"forget what lies behind and reach forward to what lies ahead"*. In other words, there are things we believe and hold on too and believe that must be replaced with God's Truth. We cannot have a change of heart about the negative things in which we believe in and embrace the truth He has for us.

Our behavior is greatly influenced by past knowledge stored within our minds. Regardless if it's positive or negative experiences, unless a person encounters Christ, his or her life will not change. Only the Spirit of the Living God can truly release a person from their emotional and mental pain.

> *Come unto me, all ye that labour and are heavy laden, and I will give you rest.*

Matthew 11:28 KJV

A HEAVY BURDEN LIFTED

During a guided prayer experience, true healing came to my soul when triggers from my past no longer controlled my life. That was the day I released several painful memories of my mother. By using a method to bring God's light to areas of my life that were dormant because of lies, false truths or mis-beliefs[1]. In the midst of my pain, God's light shined as my soul opened to discover emotional triggers of unresolved hurts. Without being aware of it, I held on to an experience of almost drowning when I was a child deep within my memory. Apparently, my older sisters were bathing me and I slipped out of their hands as bubbles were covering my head. A powerful shadow stood over them and pulled me out of the water. All these years, I had the question in my mind, "Why didn't she give me a bath?" *She* refers to my mother. I longed to have this and many more questions answered by her. Weeks later, things were still being revealed unto me.

Unfortunately, the words and memories I searched for were not there. As a child, I couldn't remember hearing words of comfort from my mother, "I love you," "I'm proud of you," "Try harder, you can do it," or "It's okay- I still love you" words like these were not part of my mother's vernacular. It's difficult for me to remember a sincere embrace from her or if I ever felt her heartbeat as I nestled near her breasts as a child. Males were the dominate figure in my life and it was males I sought out for affection. I loved my father and despite him breaking my heart we had a relationship and he communicated with me. In our time together, he shared his life experiences. Unlike my mother, I felted my father's heartbeat, as he reached out to hold me in his arms. A love I longed for and was constantly seeking.

Adding to my resume were incidents of inappropriate love and inappropriate touch, both were symbolic substitutes for my mother's unconditional love. I was betrayed by the men that were close to me. Experiencing sudden mood changes as rebellion became my new friend. I would go from family fun, hide and go seek to irritable, fresh, rude, and short-tempered. As no one was able to read my behavior or understand my emotions. I would lock myself in bathrooms and yell out to my sister *"I hate you"* in order to keep from doing my Saturday's chores, as I waited for my weekly ride to rescue me from my troubles.

There was the time my mother took me to the doctor's for a pregnancy test. Mother only wanted to confirm her suspicion, for she knew the truth. I recall sitting in the lobby, and out of nowhere, my mother asked me; "who is the father?" I couldn't believe she was that interested in knowing who the father of my child was. Besides, I was so fearful of her, I only envisioned her giving me the worst whipping of my life for telling her. Very seriously, I said these words, "I was never touched by anyone." The virgin birth was my only way out of this shameful situation. My mother looked over the top of her glasses, astonished that I could even verbalize such nonsense, but for me, it was the first time I commanded her attention.

Painful memories were still occurring for me, as I recall wearing a red and white top with white bell-bottom pants and standing near the dining room table. We were celebrating our mother's birthday when there was a loud blast, as plaster was filling the air like confetti paper on New Years. My brother had just blown a hole through the wall using Deac's double-barreled shotgun. It so happened; I was standing less than a quarter of an inch from an enormous hole in the wall, pregnant and afraid. They honestly gave more attention to the hole in the wall and my brother than my unborn child. No one even suggested that I go to the hospital. For years, I held my brother responsible for my deaf child and being emotionally traumatize.

There is a Thin Line between Love and Hate.

As I pen this, silent tears are falling from my eyes. For years, I blamed my mother for creating an atmosphere of hurt for me. I felt like my mother reached out to others in love, always helping and finding time to embrace the youth around her. Everyone called her "mom" as they expressed their love for her.

I learned to accept life as it was, a life with occasional tears of mistaken joy. That is until Jesus' radiant love and truth shined through all my pain and self-hatred to break heavy burdens and set me free. Only God can change a heart filled with guilt and shame. Unnecessary years of acting out, distorted love and misguided revenge, lead to a life filled with pain and torment. Finally, admitting in freedom, a mother's love is a powerful force in early childhood development.

Oh, I knew my mother loved me by her actions, but what I was in need of was unconditional love and natural affection. Maybe a hug or kiss would have satisfied me. It was an ongoing conflict of love and hate that caused me so much pain. A type of self-hatred every time I found myself doing the things she did or when I look in the mirror and glance her reflection as I age, which only exasperated me the more. I emotionally reacted each time someone suggested that I resembled my mother, her eyes, her walk, her hands and her demeanor. I was looking at her through my own eyes, with unresolved feelings of how she truly felt about me in her heart as a daughter, as it was my mother's reflection and love I longed for.

As the cloud of confusion lifted from my heart and mind, God's light shined in. He reminded me of the day I laid in the bed with her. My mother was diagnosis with terminal Leukemia and had a short time to live. I was reading scriptures from the book of Romans to her and for the first time, I really established a relationship with my mother. When she said to me;

"You're going to make it. You have that man who loves you. What's his name?"

"Ronald," I said.

"Okay, just tell him don't wake up and cut the grass so early people have to sleep in the morning".

That was the day I knew she loved me. She was watching me all the time. It was the only way someone would know that I love to sleep late, particularly on Saturday mornings. When did she start to notice me? I turned and smiled at her because that day, I knew she would make it to heaven. I wanted more time with her. I 'envied' to know my mother's love, but time was not on either of our side. My time with her was almost over. It was time to let her go and appreciate the way she demonstrated her love. Pain has a purpose and I was grateful to have had her as my mother.

Chapter 10
The Conflict Within Me

"*Let not sin therefore reign in your mortal body,*
that ye should obey it in the lusts thereof."

Romans 6:12 KJV

THE CONFLICT WITHIN ME

Now if we are going to overcome, we must begin inside.
God always begins there. An enemy inside the fort is far
more dangerous than one outside. Scripture teaches that in
every believer there are two natures warring against each
other. Paul says, in his epistle to the Romans, "For we know
that the law is spiritual; but I am carnal, sold under sin. For
that which I do I allow not; for what I would, that I do not;
but what I hate, that do I. If then I do that which I would
not, I consent unto the law that it is good. Now then it is no
more I that do it, but sin that dwelleth in me. For I know
that in me (that is, in my flesh), dwelleth no good thing:
for the will is present with me; but how to perform that
which is good I find not. For the good that I would I do not:
but the evil which I would not, that I do. Now if I do that
I would not, it is no more I that do it, but sin that dwelleth
in me. I find then a law, that when I would do good, evil
is present with me. For I delight in the law of God after
the inward man: but I see another law in my members,

warring against the law of my mind, and bringing me into
captivity to the law of sin which is in my members."[1]

Even knowing this my spirit remained in conflict, for mirroring my mother. In so many ways, I was like her and my mental health suffered. Exhausted from years of trying not to emulate her, then falling in the same trap! Besides, embracing was not on my to-do-list, but, if I wanted my family love, I knew my emotional envy had to change and I was determined to bring love in our lives. In order to remove envy and roadblocks, I hastily began removing items, including those things purchased that awakened silently painful memories. For it was time to line-up my spiritual, private and public life.

"A quiet mind is the life of the body, but envy is a disease in the bones."

It took an intentional effort on my part to bring my emotions to a place of peace. In the midst of many unsuccessful attempts, I commenced an eight-week journey of meaningful dialogue with the Holy Spirit to unlock years of pain and strife. I kept a journal of every feeling and negative thought. Upon discovery, my outlook on life was very cynical. I was so busy preparing to enter the kingdom through the back door of death that I failed to use the door to life, as love is the only door to the Kingdom of God, where the waters are life to the body and soul.

"Ho, every one that thirsteth, come ye to the waters, and he that hath no money; come ye, buy, and eat; yea, come, buy wine and milk without money and without price. Wherefore do ye spend money for that which is not bread? And your labor for that which satisfieth not? Hearken diligently unto me, and eat ye that which is good, and let your soul delight itself in fatness. Incline your ear, and come unto me; hear, and your soul shall live." (Isaiah 55: 1-3a KJV)

It was distorted love that blinded me from loving those dearest to me. My spiritual eyes were not enlightened to see mothers embrace their children. This time instead of envying them, a gentle smile silently appeared on my face. When the hands of the oppressor are removed, your life feels different. You are excited about a second chance at life.

My walk was not alone. It amazes me to find so many people suffering from mental health issues. People were hurting everywhere; some came into ruin by their own actions—over indulging in drugs and alcohol. There are many who are suffering from the hands of domestic violence, sexual, verbal and physical abuse. The signs of the times were present, as our children were suffering even more, because no one understands their behavior or parents silently watch as their children cycle the experiences they once did. The silent question becomes: are we powerless or are we full of Narcissistic power!

The Lord is near the broken-hearted; he is the Savior of those whose spirits are crushed down.

Having the pleasure of frequently visiting several mental health centers, it dawned on me that many were in the business of dispensing medication, there were lines, as if they were giving out hundred dollar bills. Don't get me wrong, some people need their medication. Trauma and life issues may have altered their brain chemicals to a level that hinders their psychological and emotional function. Then, there are times where we are given gifts from God to humble us, until we learn this very important life lesson, serve others.

Nevertheless, month-to-month people did not appear as if they were getting better. Speaking with my new acquaintances, many of them relied on others to solve their problems. Some were in difficult situations and were not willing to get out because of financial dependence. Several experienced job loss, troubled children and others who required emotional support. Yet, they all had one common bond, as they were encapsulated in pain. As time passed, my life took on a new meaning to understand a person's pain, regardless of one's situation and that is: At some point in life, we all need help to ease our pain.

Chapter **11**

Blessing Masquerading as Problems

"Some people ruin themselves by their own stupid actions and then blame the Lord."

Proverbs 19:3 GNT

BLESSING MASQUERADING AS PROBLEMS

Like the blind man, I wanted to be healed right there and then. Jesus, instead, takes me by the hand and takes me somewhere else, somewhere unexpected. Like the blind man, I expect Jesus' first touch to make me whole. Jesus, instead, wipes away the grime and grit first allowing me to see the root of my pain and my sinful choices. Like the blind man, I needed to be brought to Jesus by loving friends, people who didn't want me to stay the way I was. Jesus, again, shows Himself both amazingly good and incredibly sovereign in my journey towards being whole and living holy. Like the blind man, I begin to see . . . and Jesus, who is the same yesterday, today, and forever, does not leave me among the walking trees: He finishes what He starts. [1]

People are hurting, and discouraged about life. The truth is, life is not an easy task, regardless of who you are. Finding emotional support may be difficult, as one will have to trust the other. When I look beyond the surface, my life was enmeshed in controlling the lives of others. Being a healthcare manager for more than twenty-five years, had taken its toll on me, I was ready to walkout! There were constant moral issues and I didn't help for finding errors in employees' workstations. Clueless to their sufferings, I soon realized that many were finding comfort in the workplace; after all, it was healthcare.

They were a part of my life and God had entrusted them unto me, as His family. It was my duty to make things clear. The clearer things are- the happier people feel, as they were overwhelm emotionally. Life issues had them as well and they did not have the time to handle the politics of the day. Was it possible to be used by God in the workplace without preaching from the pulpit? Could God use me in the midst of my family struggles? I was far from perfect, thinking to myself, there was no way I was going to share what was happening in my home with the employees. I was the manager and mangers know how to handle *all* tough situations- Right- Wrong! God was setting me up for a higher purpose in Him.

> *Since God has so generously let us in on what he is doing, we're not about to throw up our hands and walk off the job just because we run into occasional hard times. We refuse to wear masks and play games. We don't maneuver and manipulate behind the scenes. In addition, we don't twist God's Word to suit ourselves. Rather, we keep everything we do and say out in the open, the whole truth on display, so that those who want to can see and judge for themselves in the presence of God. If our Message is obscure to anyone, it's not because we're holding back in any way. No, it's because these other people are looking or going the wrong way and refuse to give it serious attention. All they have eyes for is the fashionable god of darkness. They think*

he can give them what they want, and that they won't have to bother believing a Truth they can't see. They're stone-blind to the dayspring brightness of the Message that shines with Christ, who gives us the best picture of God we'll ever get. Remember, our Message is not about ourselves; we're proclaiming Jesus Christ, the Master. All we are is messengers, errand runners from Jesus for you. It started when God said, "Light up the darkness!" and our lives filled up with light as we saw and understood God in the face of Christ, all bright and beautiful. If you only look at us, you might well miss the brightness. We carry this precious Message around in the unadorned clay pots of our ordinary lives. That's to prevent anyone from confusing God's incomparable power with us. As it is, there's not much chance of that. You know for yourselves that we're not much to look at sometimes. We've been surrounded and battered by troubles, but we're not demoralized; we're not sure what to do, but we know that God knows what to do; we've been spiritually terrorized, but God hasn't left our side; we've been thrown down, but we haven't broken. What they did to Jesus, they do to us—trial and torture, mockery and murder; what Jesus did among them, he does in us—he lives! Our lives are at constant risk for Jesus' sake, which makes Jesus' life all the more evident in us. While we're going through the worst, you're getting in on the best! We're not keeping this quiet, not on your life. Just like the psalmist who wrote, "I believed it, so I said it," we say what we believe. Moreover, what we believe is that the One who rose up the Master Jesus will just as certainly raise us up with you, alive. Every detail works to your advantage and to God's glory: more and more grace, more and more people, more and more praise! Therefore, we're not giving up. How could we! Even though on the outside it often looks like things are falling apart on us, on the inside, where God is making new life, not a day goes by without his unfolding grace. These hard times are small potatoes compared to the coming good times, the lavish celebration prepared for us. There's far more here than meets the eye. The things we see now are here today, gone tomorrow. However, the things we can't see now will last forever. (2 Corinthians 4:1-18, Message)

"O LORD, thou art our father; we are the clay, and thou our potter; and we all are the work of thy hand."

Isaiah 64:8 KJV

About two years later, only after obeying God's voice to share my life did I see the fruit of healing. Those I thought would mock me were more compassionate, as they could not believe that someone like me would have family issues. I knew then that His glorious name was being proclaimed in the workplace. Get this; no preaching was involved, just sharing and listening to others who were in both emotional and physical pain. There were even times when sharing brought healing to my soul all because I was willing to obey the call of the Lord to share my experiences in the workplace. Pain is pain regardless of who you are! The only difference is our personal struggles manifest in different ways and on different levels.

Are we any different from the twelve Disciples of Christ? Men chosen of God, who had varied careers and went through intense training, yet soon they too found out they were human, lack understanding, and dealt with emotional barriers that prevented them from knowing their true purpose, as disciples. Again, they were human, not divine! As each of our experiences will vary from people with educational deficits, questionable backgrounds, emotionally and physically challenges. At one point in our life, emotional issues will cross all type of boundaries, regardless if you are a medical professional, social worker, educator, pastor or housewife; we all share a common bond and that's an encounter with pain and suffering.

In order to meet the challenges of today, each of us will have to stop and ask a very important question, are we willing to risk a generation from meeting the Great Physician? A doctor who guarantees to forgive, heal, and remove the stain of sin from our lives. Besides He's the only one who is intimately aware of your inner most needs and silent struggles. Society is plagued with more and more duty, as we care for aging parents, helping a family member avoid a substance abuse relapse, raising grandchildren due to parental neglect, family prison ministry and the list goes on. We all need one another's unconditional love and support.

Hurting, helpless, discouraged, depressed, frustrated, and confused, none of us has it all together and one thing is for sure we all desire and search for a better life. Our dreams are now fears of the unknown. The possibility that one would discover a dark family secret! Secrets that prevent us from reaching out to others or seeking out the help we may need. Could this be the universal dilemma? People fears are based on rejection, unhealed hurts and mistrust, thus, walls are built around their personal lives.

> *"For this reason, because we have been made servants of this new order, through the mercy given to us, we are strong: And we have given up the secret things of shame, not walking in false ways, and not making use of the word of God with deceit; but by the revelation of what is true, as before God, we have the approval of every man's sense of right and wrong. But if our good news is veiled, it is veiled from those who are on the way to destruction: Because the god of this world has made blind the minds of those who have not faith, so that the light of the good news of*

the glory of Christ, who is the image of God, might not be shining on them. For our preaching is not about ourselves, but it is about Christ Jesus as Lord, and ourselves as your servants through Jesus. Seeing that it is God who said, Let light be shining out of the dark, who has put in our hearts the light of the knowledge of the glory of God in the face of Jesus Christ. But we have this wealth in vessels of earth, so that it may be seen that the power comes not from us but from God;" (2 Corinthians 4:1-7BEE)

God's Truth cannot be found in a particular church, externals of religion or domination, it can only be found in the Word of God. It is by this that hearts and minds are changed. We as his people are to comfort the brokenhearted, cast down, and vexed in spirit. As we begin to bring down walls that divide the body, we will be able to minister hope and healing to more people who face difficult situations. Sometimes people want to be engaged with creative and innovative approaches. They want to be accepted in their as-is condition, with their flaws. Offering the gift of unconditional love as a part of the tithe will provoke change in their behaviors. After all God gave one hundred percent of himself unconditionally; He gave us his only begotten Son. God is love and He never fails to love you and me in spite of our issues. People desire change; they want to be taught how to live a victorious life. We who are strong must rise up to the call, using our spiritual gifts to counsel, guide, and lead others into the marvelous light.

Laurie Beth Jones, in her book, Jesus CEO: *Using Ancient Wisdom for Visionary Leadership wrote, "One person trained twelve human beings who went on to so influence the world that time itself is now recorded as being before or after his existence. This person worked with a staff that was totally human and not divine. A staff that in spite of illiteracy, questionable backgrounds, fractious feelings, and momentary cowardice went on to accomplish the tasks he trained them to do. They did this for one main reason to be with him again. With the world changing so rapidly and so drastically, it seemed that we need creative and innovative role models now more than ever before. The world is crying out for leaders whose goals are to build up, not to tear down; to nurture, not to exploit; to under gird and enhance, rather than dominate."[2]*

This was my opportunity to 'serve' the world and to use motivational gifts. As a light went on in my head, it was an opportunity to do both, offer the gift of Truth and educate people to serve an aging community. Recently, there has been an influx of middle age people who are suffering from chronic diseases at a greater rate than our seniors are these days. Young people now more than ever suffers with, diabetes, stroke, renal failure and HIV/AIDS, with their permission many times I am able to share with them my faith in God, as they share with me the changing times, neglect of their body and what went wrong...

At the same time, it would not please God to help others and give up on my own family. Although, the thought was very tempting, particularly when it was time to resign to challenging behaviors. Nevertheless, it was time to keep the focus on the man in the middle, as God's purpose was much higher than my understanding. It was not about me.

It was time to bring Adrian to the True Healer, as unconditionally love was now ministering in my heart. *"And they were bringing unto him little children, that he should touch them: and the disciples rebuked them. But when Jesus saw it, he was moved with indignation, and said unto them, Suffer the little children to come unto me"* (Mark 10:13-14 ASV).

This time, it was different. I was no longer tending to his emotional needs during summer break or attempting to control his behavior over the Christmas holiday. This time I understood his fears and was learning how to manage both him and his emotions. Given that, I made a decision to surround myself around positive people; especially those who were willing to help when we required a respite. It was amazing how easy it was to find solace in godly counsel, family therapy, and support groups. I resolved to a 'whatever it takes' mentality, in order to obtain a sacred balance as a sense of wellbeing was returning to our home..

Chapter 12
Children are Affected

"Children –even very young ones- are deeply affected by what transpires in their environment, and can sustain severe emotional and psychological trauma from being exposed to domestic violence. A baby or toddler- even one who is pre-verbal- may mimic abusive acts; react to noises, lights, and changes in the environment, or react in an exaggerated manner to "ordinary" separations from caregivers. A preschooler may not be able or willing to talk about the abuse she/he has witnessed, but may re-enact the experience in the play setting. A preteen may become sexually active, start smoking, become truant, or act out in other ways that appear on the surface to be 'bad behavior.' But, in reality, she/he may be manifesting intense fear and anxiety. Teenagers may replicate what they have learned at home, and become either victims or perpetrators. When dealing with a child or teenager who has been exposed to domestic violence, be a steady, firm, loving reassuring presence in his or her life. Realize (this) that a young person's misbehavior may be the result of being abused, witnessing violence, or living in an abusive household".[1]

We were living with a child who feared failure and his stress hormones were not helping the situation. In fact, it was overwhelming and yet we were not ready to give up on him.

He was mirroring his environment and he was not alone. Others his age were 'out of control' or were they? Could it be a cry for help! Now that I was emotionally connected to him, it was apparent that he was seeking my attention and that was the only means he had learned to achieve his primary need.

Is it possible that we were unknowingly signing up our children for the wrong kingdom? On the other hand, is it our own fears preventing children from entering the Kingdom of God? Our children had within them fury and rage. Internal anger that thrived on fear and the result was impulsiveness and negative behaviors. It was important that I educate and reach out to others within our community who had already traveled this journey. It was my understandings that there was a root cause to his problematic behaviors, which were merely survival techniques that prevented us from getting to the true source of his misbehavior.

"And he took them in his arms, and blessed them, laying his hands upon them."

Mark 10:16 ASV

Signs of mental and physical exhaustion were plastered across our faces, as we were being trampled from calls regarding his classroom behaviors. Over and over again, we explained his emotional and mental state. It appeared as if they were simply not listening. It wasn't personal, it was paper work. The educational staff was overwhelmed and many teachers were not able to manage emotional trauma. Emotionally, he couldn't comprehend what was going to happen from one day to the next.

At the same time, his school was my haven. The truth is we dreaded teacher workdays. Our first, Spring Break was a nightmare in itself. This poor kid was trapped in the middle of it all. There were times I couldn't image what he was feeling. He didn't belong anywhere! His summers was filled with misery as he was expelled from camp and 'normal children activities,' regardless of the director's knowledge of his background. He managed to do well for a few weeks with extensive monitoring and security from the staff; however, I say again, *"staff was simply not equipped to manage children's emotional trauma." As I prayed to God to send me helpers who loved Jesus and were full of his love and power. The more the Spirit ministered to me through his word. Love conquers all! Now it was time to fight for my family, because the devil was angry and purposely making war on my seed."* (Revelation 12:17BBE).

Wise women build their homes- social settings were another story. Since I was trained to notice errors, it was apparent that mothers were allowing their children to run free. Many never took the time to check up on their children, particularly young mothers. It was a time to relax and enjoy themselves; in the meantime, I was drafted as patrol mom.

Allowing a child to be idle and free is like sending them off to a war. Unmonitored social activities only triggered unwanted behaviors that carried on well into the week. On top of that, there were children who had more stuff than he had. Stuff like electronic games, music devices, cell phones, and name brand sneakers. Yet, they fail to answer age appropriate questions. There was something mysteriously wrong with this picture. Many times, my dear husband would relieve me of my duties, just to notice similar if not the same as I did. Although our hearts were assigned to our child, our hearts extended to the others as well, both parent and child.

At this point, my husband was ready to give up; as the pain was in my husband's eyes. He had to learn how to understand and bond with a child who suffered emotionally and he had to face issues that were coming up sometimes on a day-to-day and week-to-week basis. Nevertheless, the emotional issues were unpredictable and the strain of it all was wearing on our marital relationship and even more on our finances, which was already suffering a meltdown.

> *"But also look ahead: I'm sending Elijah the prophet to clear the way for the Big Day of GOD-the decisive Judgment Day! He will convince parents to look after their children and children to look up to their parents. If they refuse, I'll come and put the land under a curse."*
> *(Malachi 4:5-6 Message)*

We had traveled this road before and we were not about to turn our backs on him. We could no longer live in denial. Both our hearts had to care for a child that required a lot of unconditional love, attention, support, and grace. We were responsible for leading him to the Master, so he could be reconciled to God and delivered from a shattered and painful past. Mother's are a powerful force in a child's life and when we make errors in our judgments to protect our children, the results are wars breaking out and our lands cursed. Our lands are a symbol of our homes and the curse of our children's lives being shorten.

"Except the LORD build the house, they labour in vain that build it."

Psalm 127:1 KJV

Don't you see that children are God's best gift? The fruit of the womb his generous legacy? Like a warrior's fistful of arrows are the children of a vigorous youth.

Oh, how blessed are you parents, with your quivers full of children! Your enemies don't stand a chance against you; you'll sweep them right off your doorstep. All you who fear GOD, how blessed you are! How happily you walk on his smooth straight road! You worked hard and deserve all you've got coming. Enjoy the blessing! Revel in the goodness! Your wife will bear children as a vine bears grapes, your household lush as a vineyard, the children around your table as fresh and promising as young olive shoots. Stand in awe of God's Yes. Oh, how he blesses the one who fears GOD! Enjoy the good life in Jerusalem every day of your life. And enjoy your grandchildren. Peace to Israel!" (Psalm 127:3-5,128:1-6, Message)

Despite predicting behaviors, it was not enough. There was more behind all the volumes of paper, multiple diagnosis, and school incidents. Something more was happening in the inner world (heart) of this child. A world that required order! Not willing to stand idle and allow his suffering to torment him endlessly. Knowing his fears could be released to a Loving Savior. I prayed that he would send someone to help us, one who had an instrument of love and compassion in their hearts, a godly person who would build up and remove any obstacles that were standing in the midst of healing his emotional life!

One day in desperation, I was browsing the *World Wide Web* in hope of finding a resource or class that could aid us in understanding his challenging behaviors. It was as if God himself directed me to this page. A parenting class was being held in our area. Immediately, we signed up. As classes neared, the anticipation of learning how to meet his needs calmed our minds. The class merely confirmed our efforts. His behaviors were a direct result of our own unresolved issues. The class was insightful as it engaged us to understand that traditional – authoritative parenting styles were of little, if any value to a child recovering from trauma and abandonment issues. A child's only hope of healing was primarily unconditional love balanced with structure, and emotional connection. Internal reflections often eliminated reactive responses of both adult and child, as *time* was the essential ingredient in the healing process.

> *Instead of directive approaches, children with attachment challenges required innovative approaches, good listening skills and the ability to connect to the child, as the parent learn to live in forgiveness. "Parents dealing with extreme behaviors from their children often find themselves empty, depleted, and hopeless. They begin to regret their decisions to parent, they begin to feel completely incompetent, and they begin to hate their role as a parent. Ultimately, they may even reach the point of "it's either him or me who has to go." After years of living with a child who is unable to reciprocate respect, affection, and love, parent go from being a lavish rainforest of love to an arid dry desert- hostile, angry, and depleted."*[2]

Regardless of how positive you are, there comes a time when you can't manage your child's problem alone. What we needed was Truth and the truth was "help others and you will be helped." Reality suggested it would be extremely difficult to care for a child with negative behaviors, particularly one that uses manipulation as his tool for love. Emotions bumped heads when his behaviors were manifesting our minds said, return him, as if he was junk mail. On the other hand our hearts connected with him spiritually as, a sweet voice said "it's only a matter of time, there is One greater who wants to do a complete work so you maybe whole without lack."

GOD IS NOT THE AUTHOR OF CONFUSION

Parenting children with severe behaviors is not a simple job, yet it is a responsibility charged by God. It is a call to directly face our own fears, worries, and frustrations anytime those around us view our parenting struggles in a negative light, we are faced with the fear that perhaps we are not living up to the job bestowed upon us. Anytime we begin to feel as if we are ineffective parents, we are confronted with the fear of failing this calling. Moreover, any time we see that we cannot help our children make better choices and begin fearing for our children's futures as teenagers or adults, we again slip into a place of fear. This only sends us spiraling downward into our own internal negative feedback loop. Instead, we need to open ourselves up to the buttons being pushed with us by our children.... Children exhibiting severe behaviors present opportunities for us to find healing in places deep within the caverns of our hearts- dark places we never knew existed. They present us with the opportunity to make relational connections far greater than those relationships known to mankind. When a parent's heart is open and operating out of a place of love, the parent has the emotional capacity to be in the child's pain with him, instead of reacting against the child's pain and against the child. [3]

WHOSE JOB IS IT ANYWAY?

There are so many of our young people hurting. The other day a young lady in her late twenties shared her story with me (used with permission). The oldest of four, frowning and not having a problem letting me know she was angry with her parents and was moving out! "I have to tell my mother to clean up, and then when she refuses, I start to yell at her-because that's the only way she will help me around the house. Spending all her money on cigarettes and all she does is talk about her family. My parents don't even know what's good for them; if they did, they would probably do better! My mother doesn't work. All my daddy wants to do is- drink! And every six months we have to move somewhere else. Do you know how hard it is to tell your friends you don't have a place to live! I was so ashamed, especially the time we had to live in a motel. And there is nothing wrong with my mother, she can work, she just doesn't want too. Meanwhile my daddy doesn't believe he has a drinking problem. If he cared about us he would stop drinking and get help. At the rate he's drinking, he'll be dead soon! If only my mother would just get a part time job, he might not drink so much". And with one deep breathe, holding the tears from her eyes, *"Maybe they just don't care, I'm tired of paying their bills. I just can't take it anymore".*

Emotional dependency is defined as the condition resulting when the ongoing presence and/or nurturing of another is believed necessary for personal security. Emotional hurts will hinder our children from growing spiritually and insecurity will tempt them to make decisions that are emotional and hinder them spiritually from understanding their purpose in God, besides; Only a dysfunctional parent would keep his grown children at home in order to pay the bills when they are ready to marry and build a home of their own. Dependent relationships become ingrown and create a seedbed for one person to become emotionally dependent on another. [3]

Chapter 13

Standing in the Gap

There is a generation that curseth their father, and doth not bless their mother. There is a generation that is pure in their own eyes, and yet is not washed from their filthiness. There is a generation, O how lofty are their eyes! And their eyelids are lifted up. There is a generation, whose teeth are as swords, and their jaw teeth as knives, to devour the poor from off the earth, and the needy from among men.

Proverbs30:11-14, KJV

STANDING IN THE GAP

As we move toward helping our children and others in need of both spiritual and emotional guidance. There are four types of people living today: one whose relationship with God will place them in an arena to help hurting children from a distance with their financial support; Another, who will provide godly counsel and equip people to understand children fears, pains, and frustrations, then there are mature people who are willing to help remove obstacles within parent-child relationships and prepare our children to reconcile as they learn about the odds in their life; and lastly, there are a people called to keep our children's hearts and to build them up. Spiritual parents who have discernment for brokenness, these are godly people with wisdom and they are called to care for this hurting group, who long for our unconditional love.

Many children are suffering and being emotionally tormented because of physical and verbal abuse, neglect, abandonment, rejection, and lack of moral guidance. Offspring's who face enormous challenges within our society, those who have no parents, for whatever the reasons, who have unanswered questions about their life and situations. Jeremiah, the prophet, warned us that the day of spiritual parenting would come, for the evil one came in our homes through the back window, without warning. That day is now, and there must be a bridge to help our young people cross over to the other side. Who will stand in the gap for our children?

I pray for the day when young hearts will not only be restored, but reconciled to love unconditionally and forgive not only their parents, but themselves. As they learn to believe in the adults who cares for them. This generation needs men and women who are spiritually mature. Those who are called to help restore and lead them to a love Savior. Those who are not afraid to walk in their calling of parenting a generation who has experienced emotional hurts and abandoned the Truth because of society ills, environmental toxins, and learned behaviors.

> *There is a price to achieve posterity. It will cost spiritual parents to be emotionally, physically, and spiritually committed to the next generation. Yet, there are those who are chosen of God and willing to pay this personal price to raise up a new generation of sons and daughters. Nevertheless, despite any hardship on themselves, some people have matured in the things of God and resolved to advance the Kingdom of God through spiritual fathering, spiritually mentoring, and loving those who are young in the ways of the God kind of life.* [1]

As children of God, we are in a constant struggle with our identity; we input wrong thoughts and generational patterns. However, without parents, many children are left to find their own way. They have no one to help them or lead them and they have to discover life on their own, or with the help of what they are learning from television, the streets or parents who have never known the way that leads to life. The times have changed and we are living in a day where there are several generations and inter-generational families. The challenge for today's generation is how we can create an environment that allows for individuals to live out the teachings of Christ in a loving and nurturing way or without everyone so angry, that nothing is resolved and spiritual growth is not hindered. The bible is one of the oldest truths of the day and still many of us are not prepare for the times. [2]

When you leave young aggressive people to themselves without parenting, the outcome is devastating as seen in our society today. "We live in an ever-increasingly aggressive society. Anger and aggression are everywhere- on the road, on the big screen, on the news, and yes, at little league games. Children also experience aggression on a daily basis- in the classroom, in the school cafeteria, in the home with siblings, and on the playground. .. Children with trauma histories often exhibit aggressive behaviors which cannot be compared to other children in their intensity, frequency, and duration." [3]

"Hate cannot drive out hate; only love can do that."

Dr. Martin Luther King Jr.

We were learning to predict his anger, for now the time has come to keep his heart. It was like a spiritual awakening, this child felt the need to control his situations. In fact, there was some enjoyment for him. The verbal confrontations were only fueling him with negative power. There were times he couldn't wait for the verbal differences. We had to remain on a higher spiritual level in order drive out hate and discord. It appeared it was an emotionally and spiritual war raging and the conflict was within. For him, hate appeared to be clothed with love. Regardless of how I felt, being angry was a familiar place for him.

One would think a loving parent-child relationship would come naturally. Still, I didn't want to go back, our goal was to lead him to a loving Savior and our home now was beyond the conventional therapy. We were hearing the same rituals in therapy. There were so many reasons this child heart was harden. Nonetheless, we were not willing to give up on a child even if anger was now his best friend. In addition, friendship that appeared to be galvanized and proving to be very unhealthy, as well. "Anger is seen to be a friend to this child— a strong and powerful friend. Whenever the child is feeling weak, sad or any other emotion that is painful to him, the child can call upon his anger to take control of their situation. He knows that people respond to anger by getting angry back. The child is then able to control the emotional states of the people around him."[4]

Make no friendship with an angry man; and with a furious man thou shalt not go: Lest thou learn his ways, and get a snare to thy soul.

Proverbs 22:24-25 KJV

Many nights had past and his rage was somehow different. It appeared as if he was possessed by another spirit. It was like walking on eggshells in our home. What I feared, was beginning to happen. Was I learning his ways or was it in my mind (as a man thinks so is he)? What the bible declared, was happening. We were actually turning on each other. Did we doubt the healing power of the Lord? Whatever the case, it had a spiritual connection to us and how we understood him. How could we possibly love a child that tormented our home day and night with his anger- that hindered our love? The shadow of unconditional love had not fallen on me yet. It was almost impossible to love unconditional with disruptive behaviors. His fears were internal, as he dreaded being sent away to live among strangers. It would take the power of the cross to renew our strength. I cried out like the blind man, " Lord have mercy on us- please send some help from above and on earth to help us understand what was going on with this child".

In the dawn, the Lord spoke gently to me saying, "It's more than what appears on the surface". As I waited for more instructions from the Lord, nothing happened. Evening was near and there was silence once more. As a mother in labor pains, it was again time to push past my own pain, comfort and worship with a sacrifice of love. With my spirit in anticipation, the doorbell rang, the dog barked and a brother whom I misunderstood once was waiting on the other side, biding entrance to pray for my family.

A spiritual father does not have to come bearing goods and money. He can come with a willing heart to help spiritually in the time of need. Our family could always use prayer. In the physical realm, it was an opportunity for the Lord to minister so with an open heart I admitted him into our home and honored his request to pray for us. His picturesque frame reminded me so much of our father, I begin to pray that the Truth of God would manifest before his fuse shorted. Don't get me wrong, good qualities tend to live below sea level.

Something strange was mention in his prayers- he was calling out a *'deaf and dumb'* spirit and commanded the spirit to leave from this child's life, in Jesus name and never to re-enter. I was astonished! As it never occurred for me to pray in this area, both of the child's parents were deaf. God is able to see the spiritual diamond in each of us. It gave me pleasure to see that my brother cared enough about our family, that he risked laying down an emotional war between us. My brother reached out to the next generation and that was enough for me to truly let go. My brother was forgiven that day for the mishap in our life years ago at my mother's birthday celebration. It was time to restore relationships within my family as well. After his departure, there was more we should know regarding the deaf spirit, as the realities were true, they were attached to him physically and spiritually. My fears were slowing down the healing process.

Master, I have brought unto thee my son, which hath a dumb spirit; And wheresoever he taketh him, he teareth him: and he foameth, and gnasheth with his teeth, and pineth away: and I spake to thy disciples that they should cast him out; and they could not He answereth him, and saith, O faithless generation, how long shall I be with you? How long shall I suffer you? Bring him unto me. And they brought him unto him: and when he saw him, straightway the spirit tare him; and he fell on the ground, and wallowed foaming. And he asked his father, How long is it ago since this came unto him? And he said, of a child. And oft-times it hath cast him into the fire, and into the waters, to destroy him: but if thou canst do anything, have compassion on us, and help us. Jesus said unto him, If thou canst believe, all things are possible to him that believeth. And straightway the father of the child cried out, and said with tears, Lord, I believe; help thou mine unbelief. When Jesus saw that the people came running together, he rebuked the foul spirit, saying unto him, Thou dumb and deaf spirit, I charge thee, come out of him, and enter no more into him. And the spirit cried, and rent him sore, and came out of him: and he was as one dead; insomuch that many said, He is dead. But Jesus took him by the hand, and lifted him up; and he arose. He was come into the house, his disciples asked him privately, why could not we cast him out? And he said unto them, This kind can come forth by nothing, but by prayer and fasting.

(Mark 9:17-29, KJV)

The Lord is merciful and he does answers prayers. Discovering truth may come with a sacrifice of fasting, that's right turning down the steak and potatoes for a day or perhaps a month or two, mixed with an expedient prayer, gets the attention of a merciful Father. "Lord, have mercy!" It was final; Jesus alone has the power to break the bonds of the enemy. My strength was useless in the battle. A battle designed for the Lord himself. I had to admit that I barely understood the realms of demonic influence and its strongholds. I had to learn that those under the power and influence of demonic influence were in extreme pain and while medication and modern psychology explain something's, it could not explain the power of unconditional love. I know now that without believing in the power and love of Jesus in your heart nothing can be destroyed. It was time to reposition ourselves and operate in the love of Christ and believe absolutely everything in His Word without fear and doubt.

Wherefore, my beloved brethren, let every man be swift to hear, slow to speak, for the Lord is gracious, and full of compassion.... and of great mercy.

James 1:19, Psalm 145:8

You're not Listening

We were given two ears but only one mouth. The reason being— listening is twice as hard as talking. There was an urge within me that wanted to fix him and yet deep inside my heart I knew it is was God's responsibility and perfect timing to rescue him and not of my doing. Of course, that doesn't mean I have to stop listening to his concerns and deep rooted fears. I just had to learn to listen without reacting. His words exactly! "You're not listening to me." The truth is we were merely instruments of listening. The Lord was in charge of healing his hurts. The Lord was speaking to my heart with a new song- *"Put your hands in the hands of the man who heals the waters; put your hands in the hands of the man who calms the sea. Take a look at yourself and you will look at others differently. Put your hands in the hands of the man from Galilee."* His pain was slowly being replaced with peace as I was now placing him in the Lord's hands.

God was speaking and this time I was listening. The tides were returning seeds of joy as I listened to a child's view about life. There were many discoveries made the day we decided to listen. My heart was open to hear him as fears vaporized in the air. Patience was having her perfect work in our lives. What was God's plan for us? It was not until we fixed our eyes on Christ that we experience change in him and our home. We were slowly moving towards a higher dimension in trusting in a living God. It's all about the process. *"All things work together for the good for those that love the Lord."* Now, we understand what our purpose is in God and that is to care for a child in need of love and security.

Chapter 14

Stumbling Blocks

*For God's Kingdom is not a matter of eating and
drinking, but of the righteousness, peace, and joy which
the Holy Spirit gives. And when you serve Christ in this
way, you please God and are approved by others. So
then, we must always aim at those things that bring
peace and that help strengthen one another. The right
thing to do is to keep from eating meat, drinking wine,
or doing anything else that will make other believers
fall. Keep what you believe about this matter, then,
between yourself and God. Happy are those who do not
feel guilty when they do something they judge is right.*

(Romans 14:17-19, 21-22 GNT)

STUMBLING BLOCKS

Having to admit my help me blockers were on and after soul
searching my heart was open to love without conditions. There
were several warning signs of distress before this point. Needless
to say, I was caught up with my education, career, hopes, and
dreams. My idea of life was traveling summer months and long
weekends off in a remote land with my husband. Keeping the
heart of another strong willed child was not in my immediate
plans. The everyday stuff, like going to church, work, college,
vacation, and social events were my focus. Besides, there were

families torn apart when they took in a grandchild, relative or an adopted child hoping this will solve the child's issues. On my watch, I made a decision there would be no casualties, heart problems cannot be cured with housing alone. It would take more to restore this type of illness back to a healthy state. The internal workings of the child's original understanding of family must be considered if one will understand the missing links in their care and emotional dilemma.

The family systems model emphasizes the family's influence on individual behavior. This viewpoint holds that all members of a family are enmeshed in a network of interdependent roles, statuses, values, and norms. The behavior of one member directly affects the entire family system. Correspondingly, people typically behave in ways that reflect family influences. First, personality development is ruled largely by the attributes of the family, especially the way parents behave toward and around their children. Second, abnormal behavior in the individual is usually a reflection or "symptom" of unhealthy family dynamics and, more specifically, of poor communication among family members. Third, the therapist must focus on the family system, not solely on the individual, and must strive to involve the entire family in therapy. As a result, the locus of disorder is seen to reside not within the individual, but within the family system.

Inconsistent communication or distorted patterns of operation can cause children to develop a misconception of reality. The verbal content of a message can be enhanced or negated by its nonverbal content. For example, a father who insists, "I'm not angry!—While raising his voice clenching his fist, and pounding the table- is physically contradicting his verbal message. Another form of inconsistency occurs when family continually disqualify one another's messages. For example, a mother's message to her child may be negated by the father; "Your mother doesn't know what she's talking about." Such contradictions created a double bind within the child, which may result in an inability to communicate, social withdrawal, and eventually schizophrenia.[1]

NEW WINE – OLD WINE SKINS

About a year ago, my grandsons informed me, that I was doing it all wrong. Doing what wrong! "You don't know how to have fun with children— you have to learn to like what they like" Their words cut me, but you know what, I learned something that day. My parenting styles were exactly the same as before, still controlling and demanding that they follow my ways. After all, I learned my way of parenting from my mother and doing so, I failed to cultivate intimacy with them. Here I was so insistent on obedience, respect, rules and consequences that I almost pushed them away emotionally. I was no fun. Just strict! I was so busy modeling the three P's: providing, protecting, and penalizing and those restrictions were stealing my joy.

Could it be that my children were living in fear, shaped by the hands of discipline and control? Did I form their identity around a controlling mother? I realized immediately the message behind his words, seeing from the eyes of a child. That meant for me to look at life through his eyes, especially if I wanted to hold his heart in my hands. My faith fortified at that moment. God does give second chances and I am determined to be a good steward with the heart that was placed in my hands. Nevertheless, it would not be easy to win his trust or his love, his heart was well guarded by the same ills that once plagued me. That was not going to be an easy job, as unconditional love was not natural to either of us. Still it was worth the attempt.

My belief is, this generation is praying and waiting for adults to change their behaviors in the home, the work place and even the church. Coming from a reactive mode is not an easy task. It's filled with madness and unhealthiness as well; if for nothing else, do it for our children. Their challenging behaviors will cause you to reach out for help and in helping them, we will get help for our emotions in the process.

My pain has ushered me into purpose. Once I sought after the riches of this world, but now they were being stripped away. Mainly, because of stewardship errors, undue hardships, refusing to acknowledge stressors that enveloped me, and masking childhood hurts with material possessions. Oftentimes as we age, our shame and guilt grips us so firmly that our minds are held captive. Neglecting our parental responsibilities, exchanging possessions for love or failing to reach out to others when we suspect neglect, domestic violence, or abuse only add injury to an open wound. Especially, when our children challenging behaviors are impossible for us to control. Perhaps it's because as parents, we don't have the time or the energy to address the stressors that are contending for our child's attention, as well as the fact that we live in an attention deficit society. However, I must caution you that there are no simple solutions or quick fixes to the ills that are ravaging our kids. Parenting difficult children is almost an epidemic. Times are different and parenting styles must be re-evaluated, that is, if we are to keep a generation from being—all but annihilated. This is a generation that will either help us or throw our canes away. Maybe we're waiting on God's divine intervention to do what he has left for us to do. Either way, it is time for change. Regardless if you are doing a good job, single parent, fatherless, motherless, orphan, or the like, we all are human and we all need help. Whether we need help mentally, physically, emotionally or spiritually; it is time to alter our destiny by changing our current conditions.

The first thing was to look inside of me to seek change. There is a saying "rules without relationship equals rebellion." Just because I received an "F" the first time in Parenting 101, this did not declare to the world that I flunked the course. I only made mistakes along the way and now it was an opportunity to learn there is a more effective way to parent a challenged generation. There were several things to change, but it all started within me. I had to take a long look in the mirror and this time, the reflection in the mirror was not my mother, it was I. Things were changing in the world and I had to vie with peers, electronics, music videos, and all the other things of this world, particularly fast money and unnatural affection.

Chapter **15**

One Person Can Change a Family

Environment is but his looking glass.

James Allen -Author

ONE PERSON CAN CHANGE A FAMILY

Families have changed over the years and I doubt parenting styles for ten, twenty, or even five years ago, would survive in today's society. Parents are faced with tough choices and many young parents are not familiar with consequences for their unhealthy choices. A lack of education makes it difficult to manage a healthy child. One can only imagine the difficulties young parents are experiencing with a troubled child. With divorce on the rise, abuse in the news and sexual content in most of the media, we can only speculate what will happen in the future if things don't turnaround. These are only a few issues that creep in our homes unaware. Many women and children spend several nights a week in church, only to return home to violence and abuse. Our papers are filled with fallen clergy, community leaders and media personalities who fall victim to toxins of flawed mankind. Our focus must shift on a loving Savior and His relationship skills to others within our homes, communities and market places. It's time for our attitude to reflect a nevertheless mindset to the Father's will for our families, children and their children.

> *"And Jesus called a little child unto him, and set him in the midst of them, And said, Verily I say unto you, Except ye be converted, and become as little children, ye shall not enter into the kingdom of heaven. Whosoever therefore shall humble himself as this little child, the same is greatest in the kingdom of heaven. And whoso shall receive one such little child in my name receiveth me. But whoso shall offend one of these little ones which believe in me, it was better for him that a millstone was hanged about his neck, and that he were drowned in the depth of the sea." (Matthew 18:-6 KJV)*

Boy! This seems like a good time to humbly ask God for forgiveness and repent. As I pray for His blessing on my family, community and nation, that peace be upon our children's children in this lifetime.

We best care for others, by first caring for ourselves! Buzzwords were in my ears. Let it go! Talk about it and you will feel better, my listening goal was met. Like him, a child in need, I also needed to understand my feelings and resolve to a healthier way of living. My tears were arid and the mistreatment that once lingered in my thoughts was rapidly escaping my mind. Flashbacks no longer ruled my day, as I was determined to let go of the past. History was being made in my life, as I made a choice to close all the doors to my pain. Negative circumstances that engulfed me no longer held me captive. My commitment to healing was carved within my mind. I was now entrusted to the care of Jesus and His stabilizing power of the Holy Spirit. I wanted my healing to be for an eternity, with or without tribulations on earth and it started with removing all negative thoughts from my life. It was about focusing on the positives in life. My heart was new and my mind was being renewed.

> *"Be ye therefore followers of God, as dear children; and walk in love, as Christ also hath loved us, and hath given himself for us an offering and a sacrifice to God for a sweet smelling savor. For ye were sometimes darkness, but now are ye light in the Lord: walk as children of light: For the fruit of the Spirit is in all goodness and righteousness and truth Proving what is acceptable unto the Lord." Ephesians 5:1-2, 8- 10, KJV*

CHEMICAL REACTION OR PROCESS

I've learned over the years that it's common for some bacterial infections to be resistant to antibiotics. As well as, there were some antibiotics that can produce an allergic reaction. What's the point! There are some generational patterns, beliefs and systems that are so ingrained in one's mind, that new ways of doing things will have opposition before change occurs. The body naturally resists changing. In fact, some experts suggest that the body goes into shock during radical changes. That is to say, change is never trouble-free. Still there are many lessons to learn about transformation that is not visible to the naked eye. To detect even the smallest occurrence of change, it would require a microscopic tool and one day the results will eventually show up.

I believe many of our diseases, problems and issues occur out of ignorance. Merriam-Webster's define ignorance as *lack of knowledge, education, or awareness.* Whereas, generational sins are the influences of sins we know about regarding our ancestors. Generational sins may take on the cycle of alcohol, drugs, gambling, children born out of wedlock, and abuse.

Regardless if it's verbal, physical or emotional, abuse is just that—abuse!

Yes, times have altered, but we are now living in an information era and change is possible, but for some, they will need the help of others in order for their transformation to take place. It's possible that being aware is not an indication of knowing how to eradicate stressors. Some suffer unnecessarily under the fierce hands of abuse, thus their bodies and minds are worn down as they submit to the power over them. There is another group that insists on medical professionals to heal them, yet they refuse to care for their own bodies. Thus, medical dilemmas are the result of strong drinks and extravagant foods becoming their silent partners. With all the money circulating, one would think that peace of mind is merely an exhale, but not so.

None of us are perfect; however, if we are to achieve our rightful position with God, we must be determined not to allow ancestral patterns and false beliefs prevent us from keeping our children's hearts. Our minds must be recreated to its original form; however, in order for this to happen, we must trace the first family footsteps and return to the original place of creation- the *Garden of Eden*. That perfect place before deceit, blame and guilt over shadowed God's best creation- man. The Garden of Eden will forever remain a perfect place where all our needs are met by our Father in Heaven. For our children, a little more quality time and a little less stuff, one may discover that their needs are best met through unconditional love. Therefore, who needs a doctor? Jesus is the greatest physician; He is the only one who can take us to that perfect place of peace. When we live our lives between his birth and death at the cross, we will find the peace we all long for, a sanctuary where freedom is in salvation. His unconditional love for us breaks the power of the evil one. The accuser, only dwells on our wrongs and never sees any good in what we do. God's love for us is stronger than our guilt and shame. His desire is not only to heal us, but His desire, is that we could experience an abundant life; that my friend is His creative plan for our lives.

He came to heal the broken hearted; proclaim liberty to the captives, and open prison doors to those who are held enslaved in transgressions. Jesus, a loving Savior lived on this earth in a body like ours, He understands all the details of our lives and he most definitely understands all our sorrows and sufferings. It is He, along with the people that have been placed in our lives that pull us up from the pits of despair. He is well able to sympathize and empathize with us far beyond our own understanding- and that is the Truth that will set you free!

Chapter 16

Seek Counsel

"He knows our pain and our troubled heart. God does not intend to punish us in our suffering, He sent the world his son, a vision of hope and love."

SEEK COUNSEL

Without a solid anchor in God's Word, many will find themselves hard pressed to define His TRUTH. This is precisely Satan's goal, to bruise our emotions so that we may find it extremely difficult to overcome life adversities, to the point that our blindness overwhelms our spirit man leaving us helpless and defeated; as sheep going to the slaughter! God knows every detail of our lives and He refuses to leave us helpless or as victims of our circumstances. It appears that rejection is the root of almost all emotional problems and it appears that life issues have complicated things even more. Families must grasp the impact of emotional ills and its direct impact on our negative behaviors. The fight is not with the person it's with ones actions. The reality is that, maybe it's time to seek help to eradicate negative behaviors that overshadow our time, energy and emotions.

The word emotion includes a wide range of observable behaviors, expressed feelings, and changes in the body state. This diversity in intended meanings of the word emotion makes it hard to study. For many of us emotions are very personal states, difficult to define or to identify except in the most obvious instances. Moreover, many aspects of emotion seem unconscious to us. Even simple emotional states appear to be much more complicated than states as hunger and thirst. The theory of emotion as it relates to adaptive biological processes; *suggests that there are eight basic emotions grouped in four pairs of opposite and all emotions are a combination of these basic emotions: joy/sadness, acceptance/disgust, anger/fear, and surprise/anticipation.*[1]

Counseling, in a very real sense, is a study of behavior. It is teaching us to become aware of the conscious and unconscious forces which cause us to behave as we do. Life and behavior can become so routine, so taken for granted, that we feel we no longer need to observe it in action. We experience and continue to respond to the experience in precisely the same way, month-after-month, year-after-year, for a lifetime. It usually takes a great trauma to again awaken us to behavior, for us to begin to study life again. When certain problems arise with consistency, and we tend to respond to them in a similar fashion, it is well to study them as precisely as we would any scientific phenomenon we need to comprehend. For certainly human behavior is as complicated as any scientific phenomenon. Only through a conscious study of our behavior can we discover our responses, the sources of our responses, the effects of these responses upon others and the manner in which we deal with the effects [2]

It took awhile, but I finally understood what the Lord was requesting of me. Focus on the light! Brightness will come starting with the eyes of Christ, as his vision looks pass behavior and concentrates on the heart. Earlier, I mention this would not be an easy task. There is hope!-you are not alone.

CHANGE THOUGHTS- CHANGE LIVES

According to the World Health Organization (2004), 450 million people are affected by and suffer from mental, neurobiological or behavioral problems at any given time. In the years to come, this is expected to increase. Of the people who seek health services, one in four has at least one undiagnosed and untreated mental, neurobiological or behavioral disorder[3].

One day it happened! Changes were occurring in our home and for the first time his negative behaviors were no longer the focus. My reactions were less emotional and my mind stayed on the light. Don't get me wrong, his negative behaviors are not acceptable; however, important lessons were learned. We now know when he's hurting and we understand him when his needs are not being met. At that moment, our power struggles were of the past. As I felt power and control leave the premises of my mind, my brain released enough endorphins to fill a room. Shame had relinquished its power and I was no longer ashamed of behavioral issues in public places.

"Pain comes to teach us. If we become frustrated, we've lost the lesson. When we see pain as having a purpose in life, it drives us closer to our dreams."

Art Berg -Author

ACCEPTING THE CALL

A family is a co-therapist and a partner in care, and they have ideas. Even the families who have a high commitment and who are taking good care of their affected member feel the need to be relieved of the stress of care for short periods, to avoid burnout. They encounter different problems at different stages. Stress may take many forms—demands of daily care, lack of leisure time, emotional disturbances such as worries, frustrations, sadness, irritability, and relationship problems between family members. In addition, there is stigmatization, social embarrassment, and financial implications. However, families are not always passive sufferers. They make efforts to overcome the difficulties and try to cope and adjust to the situation. They try to solicit support and advice from relatives, friends, religious persons, and professionals. In this process of adjustment, certain things help the families to cope and adapt well. Families need to gather the right kind of information about the condition and become knowledgeable about it. It is also very important for families to preserve their own health, maintain family cohesion and harmonious relations. They should try as much as possible to continue with their normal life. They should not cut off their relationships and contacts with friends and relatives out of a sense of shame or embarrassment. The burden of care should not fall only on the mother; other family members should also share in the caring. Families have a greater chance of succeeding in solving the problems when they work with a sense of togetherness. Families can sometimes bring about big changes in the society.[4]

Healing trauma is about keeping our children safe. By involving those who love them to be sensitive to their needs and by monitoring their own reactions. Temperance requires one to maintain their self-control. One of the highest orders of man is his ability to self-regulate his emotions. Had it not been for the pain in my life, I would not have endured this test. God put me in the press and squeezed new life and gave me new wine as well, his Holy Spirit. *Change truly comes from the inside out.* My grandchildren challenged me that day. Having fun with them is more important than my public image. I value them as individuals and I'm not willing to let others put the pressure on me to make them robots, given that we live in an attention deficit society.

NO GREATER LOVE

How could *One* love the world so much, that he reached deep within himself and brought forth *love.* When I think of our creation and our purpose to rule, subdue and reign over the creatures and the land, it makes me feel broken hearted to know God's best creation prefers to rule each other without using the gift that was freely given to each of us-love. For years, I've called wrong- right and right- wrong and cut hearts at the same time.

It's time to pass the mantle as we teach our children the way of the Lord and pray that they will not turn away from God's love. Yes, there will be some mistakes, because there is always room for growth. We may even fail a test or two, but this one thing I know an **"F"** no longer means that we are a defeated foe. F is for *fresh!* It's a new way of doing things. The songwriter Johnny Nash says it best:

I can see clearly now, the rain is gone,
I can see all obstacles in my way
Gone are the dark clouds that had me blind
I think I can make it now, the pain is gone
All of the bad feelings have disappeared

When the dark clouds of despair have been lifted and the love of God shines in your heart, that's when you know you are free. For whom the Son of man set free is free in deed. I was running from the reflection in the mirror, a strong determined woman, my mother. One who shared her love with everyone and touched so many lives, too many to number. Nowadays, when someone comments of her to me, smiling, I'll show him or her my hands, because now I know how deeply she loved me. Mama, I'll always love you for your prayers and for looking beyond my behaviors. Your spiritual vision held me closely under microscopic surveillance and for that, my heart is forever grateful.

Chapter 17

Leading Like the Leader

"One generation passeth away, and another generation cometh: All things are full of weariness; man cannot utter it: the eye is not satisfied with seeing, nor the ear filled with hearing. That which hath been is that which shall be; and that which hath been done is that which shall be done: and there is no new thing under the sun. There is no remembrance of the former generations; neither shall there be any remembrance of the latter generations that are to come, among those that shall come after."

Ecclesiastes 1: 4a, 8, 9, 11,KJV

LEADING LIKE THE LEADER

A mother's love is what builds a healthy home; therefore, Jesus must be the cornerstone of our lives. Each of us have to make a choice to impact and influence our children, families, homes, communities, churches, market places, and the world. Until we practice putting God's standards and principles into our homes, our children will only become better acquainted with society's evils. As many families are desperately searching for hope, the

Good News Gospels advocates that hurting and broken people crave for change. They long for a conversion that shifts them from hope to restoration. A model that directs us to what we've lost — love. There is only one Life Leader—Christ.

Go – do likewise! Leading like Jesus, is a method that challenges you to embrace the values of Christ, by assessing your goals, motives, and behaviors. It also, assesses your ability to mirror the principles of compassion and grace for those in need, our posterity.

It's unfortunate that parents do not focus on their children, providing the one-to-one instruction guide Jesus modeled to his disciples. A great deal of frustration could be eliminated if parents would lead by the example of "do likewise" as they follow the command to, Love the Lord your God with all your heart and all your soul and with all your mind and with all your strength. Leading like Jesus is vital for the family, because in Him we are forgiven. In Him, we have faith and experience the love of the Father, who is well acquainted with all our sorrows and pain. In His blood, we achieve freedom and offered Salvation. In His resurrection, we are assigned to our royal position as His heirs. This is our ultimate purpose to lead our family to the finish work at the cross.[1]

HAVE FAITH IN GOD

Keep your focus on the Man in the middle, for it's by His stripes we are restored to health. God's perfect love has a way to heal our pains and ease our fears. He alone meets our unmet needs. It is His love that's unconditional. I invite you to the fountain of living waters, where His Spirit transforms even disturbed minds. God has sent His Son, so that we may find peace. No person is trapped forever within his or her experiences. He so patiently waits for us to surrender every one of our hurts to him. Our Father's love will give us peace that exceeds all our understanding.

We have wasted enough time already. Now it's our season to stand on the promises and blessings of God. If not for your freedom, do it for our children, so that they may tell their children's children that the Lord God Almighty reigns.

HIS WAY IS A GUARANTEE

"Now, if you will be careful to obey the Lord your God and follow all his commands that I tell you today, then the Lord your God will put you high above all the nations on earth. If you will obey the Lord your God, then all these blessings will come to you and be yours: "The Lord will bless you in the city and in the field. The Lord will bless you and give you many children. He will bless your land and give you good crops. He will bless your animals and let them have many babies. He will bless all your calves and lambs. The Lord will bless your baskets and pans {and fill them with food}. The Lord will bless you at all times in everything you do. "The Lord will help you defeat your enemies that come to fight against you. Your enemies will come against you one way, but they will run away from you seven different ways!

"The Lord will bless you and fill your barns. He will bless everything you do. The Lord your God will bless you in the land that he is giving you. The Lord will make you his own special people, like he promised. The Lord will do this if you follow the Lord your God and obey his commands. Then all the people in that land will see that you are called by the name of the Lord. And they will be afraid of you. "And the Lord will give you many

good things. He will give you many children. He will give your cows many calves. He will give you a good harvest in the land that the Lord promised your ancestors to give you. The Lord will open his storehouse where he keeps his rich blessings. The Lord will send rain (Those that are full of wisdom, counselors full of the Spirit and teachers to show you the way) at the right time for your land. The Lord will bless everything you do. You will have money to lend too many nations. And you will not need to borrow anything from them. The Lord will make you be like the head, not the tail. You will be on top, not on the bottom. This will happen if you listen to the commands of the Lord your God that I tell you today. You must carefully obey these commands. You must not turn away from any of the teachings that I give you today. You must not turn away to the right or to the left. You must not follow other gods to serve them." (Deuteronomy 28 1-14 ERV)

God never required for us to be perfect; however, He does require us to obey and follow His greatest commandment–LOVE. For love never fails! And in His love is the ultimate cure and unexpected blessings.

May peace, love and the oil of Joy make your life complete in Him!

Dare and Dream
By Dr. Deborah L. Jones-Allen 2006

Promise yourself, and be persuaded in your heart that you are more than a conqueror, so that your life may be compared to golden apples served on a silver platter. Therefore, guard what you put in your spirit, on your body and think about so that nothing disturbs your peace. Your experiences tell your story. It did not make you weak; the past made you stronger in your faith walk with God. So, celebrate other's success, as if they were your own. You are unique, talented, gifted and creative. You are called to love not envy, to celebrate and live a life of victory. You must believe in God the creator of heaven and earth, and that He will give you the desires of your heart and make all your plans succeed. Go ahead, **Dare and Dream.**

Dream to live among the stars and even if you fall, you will land in the arms of loving clouds. And there will be times you may have to cry, and then your tears will fall like rain to water the earth below. So, fly with the eagles and run with the wind. You have hidden treasures buried within. You have power and value and this will make your dreams all possible, as you discover truth, self and strength, you never knew was within you. Hidden within are possibilities, your thoughts and creativity adds wisdom to your character. Because, where you are now in life, is not your final destination, it's just a stop for you to rest, as time waits for you. For the time has come for you to **Dare and Dream** again.

The whole earth is awaiting your arrival and many have been waiting before you were born. You are fairer than the children of men are; graciousness is poured upon your lips; therefore, God has blessed you forever. Our Father, call Him Dad if you wish, He has declared to the world that you are fearfully and wonderfully made. You are his workmanship— a master design in His eyesight. He formed you and covered you with His love before placing you in your mother's womb. So, let no man deceive you. You were born an original, destine for greatness as His heir. For the Lord your God knows the plans He has for you, plans to prosper you and keep harm from you. The Spirit- Himself testifies that you are his child and his heir. For He is Lord of all! He knows all about your thoughts, ideas and fears. He predestined you and created you in his image. Let His mind be in you. Your victory is in Christ the true Son. Surely, you know that God causes all things to work together for the good especially for those who love Him. If God is for you, who can be against you! So don't get tired and give up, for the race is not given to the swift, but unto the one who endures until the end and this must be you.

Acknowledgements

None of this would be possible without family, friends and mentors sharing and imparting wisdom and knowledge in my life. Elders like Roxie Greer, Daisy Harven, Robert and Margaret Allen and Mr. David Williams. Thank you for embracing me and sharing your lifetime experiences, in efforts to strengthen an entire village. William, Janet, Janice, Edward, Edward Fitzgerald and Mark, we have come this far by faith and stand on the power of our mother's prayers. To my children all of you have exceeded every expectation of a parent in a chaotic society and for that, we are grateful.

To my grandchildren and godchildren, this one is for you, thank you for keeping me focus on having fun and teaching me how to be a grandma. Neal Kjos, my mentor, your reflection of wisdom is like finding a golden pearl in a sea of affirming love, your words of wisdom have impacted my life, humbled and challenged me to try new methods in a changing and complex world in the marketplace. Your compassion for truth and family has allowed me to care for the next generation, especially when I felt like tossing in the towel during the difficult seasons of my life. Gloria Ross-Hill, Lynette Davis, Sandra Epps, Delores Dorsett, Watson and Yvonne Belidor and Barbara Wooten, God has blessed you with an anointing ear to hear as I shared my troubles with you. Thank you for all your wise counsel.

To my spiritual family Apostle Veronica Graham, thank you for opportunity, Pastors Ranzer A. and Rhonda M. Thomas and the entire New "G" Generation family for your prayers, encouraging words and affirmations in times of uncertainty. Radha Maragh, Beverly White and Jackie Townsend, the most inspiring people I have ever encountered in the workplace. To Hopie Hutchinson and Peggy Bradley for your time, talent and treasures, thank you for investing in this work. Finally, to all my spiritual sons and daughters, THANK YOU all for coming into my life and keeping it real with me and finding the courage in your hearts to embrace Truth. Always, remember, "Now is not your final destination its part of your journey— the journey of L.I.F.E. Therefore, *love* unconditionally, *influence* others with your presence, *forgive* yourself and be forgiven, and *endure* difficult moments in this lifetime. The entire earth is in anticipation of your arrival. Take your position, as it's time to transform nations, as you prepare the way for our Lord's return- whenever that may be!

Appendix **A**
Scriptures

ISAIAH 55:1-7 *(BEE Version)*

THE GREAT INVITATION OF MERCY

Ho! Everyone in need, come to the waters, and he who has no strength, let him get food: come, get bread without money; wine and milk without price. Why do you give your money for what is not bread, and the fruit of your work for what will not give you pleasure? Give ear to me, so that your food may be good, and you may have the best in full measure. Give ear, and come to me, take note with care, so that your souls may have life: and I will make an eternal agreement with you, even the certain mercies of David. See, I have given him as a witness to the peoples, a ruler and a guide to the nations. See, you will send for a nation of which you had no knowledge, and those who had no knowledge of you will come running to you, because of the Lord your God, and because of the Holy One of Israel, for he has given you glory. Make search for the Lord while he is there, make prayer to him while he is near: Let the sinner give up his way, and the evil-doer his purpose: and let him come back to the Lord, and he will have mercy on him; and to our God, for there is full forgiveness with him.

Ezekiel 18—*Message Translation*

ONE CAN CHANGE HIS WAYS AND LIVE

GOD's Message to me: "What do you people mean by going around the country repeating the saying, the parents ate green apples, and the children got stomachache? "As sure as I'm the living God, you're not going to repeat this saying in Israel any longer. Every soul—man, woman, child—belongs to me, parent and child alike. You die for your own sin, not another's. "Imagine a person who lives well, treating others fairly, keeping good relationships doesn't eat at the pagan shrines, doesn't worship the idols so popular in Israel, doesn't seduce a neighbor's spouse, doesn't indulge in casual sex, doesn't bully anyone, doesn't pile up bad debts, doesn't steal, doesn't refuse food to the hungry, doesn't refuse clothing to the ill-clad, doesn't exploit the poor, doesn't live by impulse and greed, doesn't treat one person better than another, But lives by my statutes and faithfully honors and obeys my laws. This person who lives upright and well shall live a full and true life. Decree of GOD, the Master.

"But if this person has a child who turns violent and murders and goes off and does any of these things, even though the parent has done none of them—eats at the pagan shrines, seduces his neighbor's spouse, bullies the weak, steals, piles up bad debts, admires idols, commits outrageous obscenities, exploits the poor "-do you think this person, the child, will live? Not a chance! Because he's done all these vile things, he'll die. And his death will be his own fault. "Now look: Suppose that this child has a child who sees all the sins done by his parent. The child sees them, but doesn't follow in the parent's footsteps—doesn't eat at the pagan shrines, doesn't worship the popular idols of Israel, doesn't seduce his neighbor's spouse, doesn't bully anyone, doesn't refuse to loan money, doesn't steal, doesn't refuse food to the hungry, doesn't refuse to give clothes to the ill-clad, doesn't live by impulse and greed, doesn't exploit the poor. He does what I say; he performs my laws and lives by my statutes.

"This person will not die for the sins of the parent; he will live truly and well. 18But the parent will die for what the parent did, for the sins of– oppressing the weak, robbing brothers and sisters, doing what is dead wrong in the community.

"Do you need to ask, 'so why does the child not share the guilt of the parent?' "Isn't it plain? It's because the child did what is fair and right. Since the child was careful to do what is lawful and right, the child will live truly and well. The soul that sins is the soul that dies. The child does not share the guilt of the parent, nor the parent the guilt of the child. If you live upright and well, you get the credit; if you live a wicked life, you're guilty as charged.

"But a wicked person who turns his back on that life of sin and keeps all my statutes, living a just and righteous life, he'll live, really live. He won't die. I won't keep a list of all the things he did wrong. He will live. Do you think I take any pleasure in the death of wicked men and women? Isn't it my pleasure that they turn around, no longer living wrong but living right–really living? "The same thing goes for a good person who turns his back on an upright life and starts sinning, plunging into the same vile obscenities that the wicked person practices. Will this person live? I don't keep a list of all the things this person did right, like money in the bank he can draw on. Because of his defection, because he accumulates sin, he'll die.

"Do I hear you saying, "That's not fair? God's not fair!?' "Listen, Israel. I'm not fair? You're the ones who aren't fair! If a good person turns away from his good life and takes up sinning, he'll die for it. He'll die for his own sin. Likewise, if a bad person turns away from his bad life and starts living a good life, a fair life, he will save his life. Because he faces up to all the wrongs he's committed and puts them behind him, he will live, really live. He won't die. And yet Israel keeps on whining, "That's not fair! God's not fair.' "I'm not fair, Israel? You're the ones who aren't fair. "The upshot is this,

Israel: I'll judge each of you according to the way you live. So turn around! Turn your backs on your rebellious living so that sin won't drag you down. Clean house. No more rebellions, please. Get a new heart! Get a new spirit! Why would you choose to die, Israel? I take no pleasure in anyone's death. Decree of GOD, the Master. "Make a clean break! Live!"

Appendix **B**

Notes

FCAT-The Florida Comprehensive Assessment Test® **(FCAT)** is part of Florida's overall plan to increase student achievement by implementing higher standards. The FCAT, administered to students in Grades 3-11, consists of criterion-referenced tests (CRT) in mathematics, reading, science, and writing, which measure student progress toward meeting the Sunshine State Standards (SSS) benchmarks.

Reactive Attachment Disorder (RAD) is a mental health disorder in which a child is unable to form healthy social relationships, particularly with a primary caregiver. Often children with RAD will seem charming and helpless to outsiders, while waging a campaign of terror within the family. RAD is frequently seen in children who have had inconsistent or abusive care in early childhood, including children adopted from orphanages or foster care. Physical, emotional, social, mental, and spiritual health are all affected by RAD (Post 2001).

SYMPTOMS AND CAUSES OF ATTACHMENT DISORDERS

Symptoms

Intense control battles, very bossy and argumentative; defiance and anger

Resists affection on parental terms

Lack of eye contact, especially with parents—will look into your eyes when lying

Manipulative—superficially charming and engaging

Indiscriminately affectionate with strangers

Poor peer relationships

Steals

Lies about the obvious

Lack of conscience—shows no remorse

Destructive to property, self and/or others

Lack of impulse control

Hypervigilant/Hyperactive

Learning lags/delays

Speech and language problems

Incessant chatter and/or questions

Inappropriately demanding and/or clingy

Food issues—hordes, gorges, refuse to eat, eats strange things, and hides food

Fascinated with fire, blood, gore, weapons, evil

Very concerned about tiny hurts but brushes off big hurts

Parents appear hostile and angry

The child was neglected and/or physically abused in the first three years of life

Potential Causes

Neglect

Abuse

Separation from the primary caregiver

Changes in the primary caregiver

Frequent moves and/or placements

Traumatic experiences

Maternal depression

Maternal addiction—drugs or alcohol

Undiagnosed, painful illness such as colic, ear infections

Lack of attunement between mother and child

Young or inexperienced mother with poor parenting skills

Adapted from Post (2001) Post Institute for Family Centered Therapy:

Theophostic Prayer Ministry: Theo (God) Phostic (light) is a ministry of prayer that is Christ-centered and God-reliant for its direction and outcome. Simply stated, it is encouraging a person to discover and expose what he believes that is a falsehood; and then encouraging him to have an encounter with Jesus Christ through prayer, thus allowing the Lord to reveal His truth to the wounded person's heart and mind. It is not about advice giving, diagnosing problems, or sharing opinions or insight. It is about allowing a person to have a personal encounter with the Lord Jesus in the midst of the person's emotional pain. Dr. Ed M Smith is the founder of Theophostic Prayer Ministries.

References

Chapter One

[1] The Florida Comprehensive Assessment Test® (FCAT). http://fcat.fldoe.org, September 2008

[2] Post (2001) Post Institute for Family Centered Therapy: If you want to learn more about Reactive Attachment Disorder and the Effects of Early Child Hood Trauma, we recommend Trauma Brain and Relationship.info@postinstitute.com

[3] James Allen, *As a Man Thinketh,* (DeVorss & Company, Camarillo CA). p.31. www.devorss.com

Henry, Matthew. "Complete Commentary on Jeremiah 29". "Matthew Henry Complete Commentary on the Whole Bible". http://www.studylight.org/com/mhc-com/view.cgi?book=jer& chapter=029. 1706.

Chapter Four

Carter, Les.Ph.D, Putting the Past Behind, Biblical solutions to your unmet needs. (Moody Press, Chicago, 1989), p.16-17.

Webster Ninth New Collegiate Dictionary, Merriam –Webster Inc., 1991,

Chapter Five

Barnet, Ann B, and Richard J., MD, *The Youngest Minds, Parenting and Genes in the Development of Intellect and Emotion:* Language of the Heart, (Simon & Schuster 1998), p. 107-110.

Villoldo, Alberto, Ph.D., *Mending the Past and Healing the Future with Soul Retrieval,* (Hay House, Inc Carlsbad, Ca, 2005), www.hayhouse.com, p. 126-127

Chapter Six

[1]Barnet, Ann B, and Richard J., MD, *The Youngest Minds, Parenting and Genes in the Development of Intellect and Emotion; Children's Anger and Adult Violence.* (Simon & Schuster 1998) p. 142-3

[2] *ibid* p.144-47

Villoldo, Alberto,Ph.D., *Mending the Past and Healing the Future with Soul Retrieval,* (Hay House, Inc Carlsbad, Ca, 2005) www.hayhouse.com, p. 126-127

[3] Barnet, Ann B, and Richard J., MD, *The Youngest Minds, Parenting and Genes in the Development of Intellect and Emotion, Children's Anger and Adult Violence* (Simon & Schuster 1998) p.135

[4] Step by Step, A Guide for working the steps of Emotions Anonymous, p 9

[5] Emotions, Anonymous, International, P.O. Box 4245, St Paul MN 55104-0245, www.eameeting.org

[6] Alcoholics Anonymous®, *Women Suffer Too: Alcoholics Anonymous World Services,* Inc, (New York City. 1976) p.226-229

Chapter Seven

Buscaglia, Leo, *Love, Fawcett Crest,* (Ballantine Books, New York, 1972) p. 82-84

John Piper, *Seeing and Savoring Jesus Christ. Desiring God's Foundation.* (Crossway Books. Wheaton, Illinois, 2004. 1972) p. 15

Chapter Eight

Berg, Art, *The Impossible Just Takes A little Longer.*(HarperCollins Publishers, New York, NY. 2002). p.71

Barnet, Ann B, and Richard J., MD, *The Youngest Minds, Parenting and Genes in the Development of Intellect and Emotion. Children's Anger and Adult Violence.* (Simon & Schuster 1998). p. 191-205

[2] ibid p. 142-3

Chapter Nine

Theophostic Prayer Ministry: Theo (God) Phostic (light) is a ministry of prayer that is Christ centered and God reliant for its direction and outcome. Simply stated, it is encouraging a person to discover and expose what he believes that is a falsehood; and then encouraging him to have an encounter with Jesus Christ through prayer, thus allowing the Lord to reveal His truth to the wounded person's heart and mind. It is not about advice giving, diagnosing problems, or sharing opinions or insight. It is about allowing a person to have a personal encounter with the Lord Jesus in the midst of the person's emotional pain. Dr. Ed M Smith, founder. Theophostic Prayer Ministries. http://www.theophostic. com/content.asp?ID=2. November.28.2008

Chapter Ten

Moody, Dwight L., *The Overcoming Life,* (Moody Press, Chicago,1995) p.17

Chapter Eleven

[1] Luke Gilkerson, *Brain Chemicals, Kirk Franklin, and Walking Trees, Will Jesus Heal Me of My Addiction,* (Posted on: January 24th, 2008). http://www.covenanteyes.com/blog/2008/01/24/brain-chemicals-kirk-franklin-and-walking-trees/: Adapted April 7, 2009

[2] Laurie Beth Jones, *Jesus CEO, Using Ancient Wisdom for Visionary Leadership,* (Hyperion, New York, 1995) p. XIII-XIV

Chapter Twelve

[1] The Soul Sanctuary; Interfaith Clergy Advisory Council, Toolkit for Responding to Domestic Violence in Communities of Faith, (Chicago Metropolitan Battered Women's Network, Chicago, IL, 2005) www.batteredwomensnetwork.org, p 25

[2] Heather Forbes, LCSW ,& Bryan Post PhD, *Beyond Consequences, Logic and Control; A Love-based Approach to Helping children with severe Behaviors.* (Beyond consequences Institute, LLC , Orlando, Fl.copyright©2006) If you would like to learn more about parenting and therapy for children with early life trauma and attachment issues, www.Beyondconsequences.com p. 33

[3] ibid. p. 38-40.

[4] Larry Kreider, *A Cry for Spiritual Fathers & Mothers,* (House to House Publications, Ephrata, Pennsylvania, 2000). p. 69,118. Book Review- Ministerial Studies. 2007

Chapter Thirteen

[1] ibid Book Review, Ministerial Studies. 2007

[2] ibid. Book Review, Ministerial Studies. 2007

[3] Heather Forbes, LCSW, & Bryan Post PhD, *Beyond Consequences, Logic and Control;* A Love-based Approach to Helping children

with severe Behaviors.(Beyond consequences Institute, LLC , Orlando, Fl.copyright©2006.) If you would like to learn more about parenting and therapy for children with early life trauma and attachment issues, www.Beyondconsequences.com. p.66

[4] ibid. p. 67

Chapter Fourteen

[1] Sue, David. Sue, Derald. Sue, Stanley. Understanding Abnormal Behavior. 5thed. (Houghton Mifflin Company. Boston, New York.1997). p.56-8

Chapter Sixteen

[1] Psychology of Behavior, *What is Emotion,* http://library. thinkquest.org/26618/en-1.4.1=What%20are%20emotions. htm (Plutchik, R. (1980). A general psycho evolutionary theory of emotion; Relation to adaptive biological processes) 10/1/08

[2] Buscaglia, Leo, Ph.D., *The Disabled & Their Parents; A Counseling challenge* (Slack Incorporated, Thorofare, New Jersey; Holt, Rienehart and Winston, New York, 1983, New York) p. 213

[3] SMHAI- Suicide and Mental Health Association International- Mental Health Basics- http:// suicideandmentalhealthassociationinternational.org/index.html, 10/1/08

[4] *Mental Health and Substance Abuse, Family Stress and Adaptation*: http://www.searo.who.int/en/Section1174/Section1199/ Section1567/Section1825_8107.htm 10/1/08

Johnny Nash—*I Can See Clearly Now Lyrics*- http://www.stlyrics. com/lyrics/hardertheycome/icanseeclearlynow.htm

Chapter Seventeen

[1]Ken Blanchard and Phil Hodges, *Lead Like Jesus,* (W Publishing Group, Thomas Nelson, Inc. Nashville, TN, 2005) Book Review Ministerial Studies .2007

Internet Bible verses taken from http://www.studylight.org

About the Author

Dr. Deborah Jones-Allen is the Founder and Director of Daughters of Siyyon, a Chartered Counseling Ministry of the National Conservative Christian Church. She is a Licensed and Ordained Minister receiving a Ph.D. in Clinical Pastorral Counseling and Doctoral or Ministry in Christian Counseling, as well as a Masters of Business Administration. She has over 25 years in Health Care Management.

Dr. Allen is a native of Miami, Florida and resides with her loving and supportive husband for over 14 years, Ronald Allen. Together, they have seven children and eight grandchildren. She writes about her personal journey of overcoming childhood abuse, low self-esteem, rejection, and personal family struggles, which led her to pursue a career in Christian psychology.

Dr. Allen's strongest passion is in aiding children who need restoration through emotional healing. A restoration that is paramount, in order for today's generation to experience freedom, wholeness and salvation in Christ Jesus, particularly those who fear rejection. She is a Christian Life Coach, motivational and inspirational speaker. Dr. Allen is positioned to fulfill her destiny under the healing anointing of our Lord and Savior Jesus Christ.

Book Summary
Mirrored Reflection

This book is an *Emotional Experience to Unleash Pain, Hope, and Determination.* At first, it was very difficult for me to express in words, especially in writing, deep secrets that were embedded with shame, guilt, and internal fears. Before divine intervention helped me understand that childhood hurts are just that-childhood hurts; I was continuously engulfed in a battle that raged war between my spirit, soul, and body. If these hurts are left untreated or unaddressed, these childhood hurts have the potential of developing into an array of unwelcomed personality disorders, emotional problems, and physical illnesses that interferes with one's education, relationships, finances, and spirituality.

Regardless if your pain is emotional, physical, or verbal, failure to seek help only results in emotional pain that cycles brokenness that advances to the next generation. Sadly, human behaviors are often altered by society ills, toxic environments and learned behaviors, which deepens internal conflicts.

When a person recognizes that good is within them, they are able to see themselves differently. In order for many of us to move forward, we will have to journey back, a trip that goes far beyond one's immediate family, circumstances and painful memories. As recorded in the book of Genesis, the journey oftentimes must go back to the footsteps of the first family; it is there, that one will find blame, guilt and shame, in the midst of paradise- a place of peace and love. It is here, where we can accept and understand the meaning of being created in God's image-to mirror His presence in the earth. Despite life adversities, you can live a victorious life by knowing that Christ is in control of your life. In this book, Mirrored Reflection, you will experience my pain and my determination to love and to be loved as I embraced the Blessed Hope.

www.ingramcontent.com/pod-product-compliance
Lightning Source LLC
Chambersburg PA
CBHW020853090426
42736CB00008B/361